THE HOLY RIVER OF GOD

CURRENTS AND CONTRIBUTIONS OF THE WESLEYAN HOLINESS STREAM OF CHRISTIANITY

WESLEYAN
HOLINESS
CONNECTION

BARRY L. CALLEN

Editor

ALDERSGATE
PRESS

THE HOLY RIVER OF GOD
CURRENTS AND CONTRIBUTIONS OF THE
WESLEYAN-HOLINESS STREAM OF CHRISTIANITY

Barry Callen, Editor

ALDERSGATE **PRESS**
THE PUBLICATIONS ARM OF

WESLEYAN
HOLINESS
CONNECTION

HolinessandUnity.org

In Collaboration with

LAMP POST inc.
www.lamppostpublishers.com
Spring Valley, CA

Printed in the United States of America

Soft Cover ISBN 13:   978-1-60039-309-9
ebook ISBN-13:   978-1-60039-981-7
Library of Congress Control Number: 2016955616

DEDICATION

For Jan, my wife and best friend,
through whom much grace
and holy love from God
have flowed into
my life.

There is a river whose streams make glad the city of God,
the holy place where the Most High dwells. God is within
her, she will not fall; God will help her at break of day.

(Psalm 46:4-5)

There is a precious river where God dwells;
It will endure and minister for all time;
God is helping its flow in this new day.
The WHC is an instrument of that flow.

CONTENTS

Section III: THE STORY OF THE WESLEYAN HOLINESS CONNECTION • 141

WHC NETWORKS

WHC ASSOCIATED MINISTRIES

Section IV: WHC RESOURCE DOCUMENTS ON TODAY'S CRITICAL ISSUES • 223

INTRODUCTION

God is on the move in our time! The Holy One is wanting and enabling a holy people who are willing to be instruments of cleansing in our deeply distorted world. Christians are not being called to be fanatical extremists but humbled and holy servants full of good news about love, liberation, forgiveness, community, justice, and unity. We are to be nurturing seeds from above that can flower into a new day for humanity – if only we will listen, receive, and obey. We are to become a strong current in the River of God flowing into the dryness of our times.

A Strong Current in the Divine River

The Wesleyan Holiness Connection (WHC) is a growing network of Christians seriously seeking to listen, receive, and obey. The WHC is more a contemporary movement of God than just another organization within the life of today's larger church. It is spontaneous gatherings of like-minded believers from many denominations and nations. While this network has come to have the WHC name, its core intention and motivating reality has been . . . **W**ith **H**oliness **C**entral.

Holinessandunity.org is more than the web address of the WHC. It's the dynamic that is offering fresh hope to the Christian community, and through it to the world. We believers in Jesus are finding ourselves truly together as God's one family on mission when we share through Christ the transforming life of God's one Spirit.

The history of Christianity admittedly is a mixed bag, and the present challenges before it are great. One thing that sometimes has infected the holiness stream of Christianity, and currently troubles Western societies in general, is *individualism*. Holiness gets reduced to private spiritual experiences and localized morality rules. However, the "Wesleyan" theological roots of the WHC push hard against such distortions, as does the community-of-faith aspect of the biblical revelation itself.

The WHC intends to be a conscious community within the holiness stream of God's rushing river, one way that the wholeness of this critical heritage can be championed today. Its participants know that more adequate understanding and effective church mission exist when they are together than when they function in isolation from each other, lacking each other's experience and wisdom.

The several dimensions of the life of the WHC, and thus the organizing pattern of this book, are three, namely:

> One. The reality of a powerful stream in the River of God, the Holiness stream, that is deep in biblical revelation and in various forms has been constantly present in all of church history.

> Two. The numerous facets of this holiness gem that appear in the heritages of the several denominations that have claimed and are highlighting the biblical holiness now seeking to stream God's life to us thirsty humans.

> Three. The significant practical relevance of this stream of holiness as the body of Christ seeks to face and address the many difficult issues facing the church and its mission in today's culture.

What is the Holiness Stream?

It must be faced with humility and courage. There is a trail of distortions to be overcome. Holiness teaching and living among Christians too often have become burdened by outdated religious language, culturally-defined rather than Christ-defined practices, and individualistic reductions of the whole truth.[1]

Seeking to be as free of such things as possible, we now ask this. What is authentic Christian holiness? The following is an excellent place to begin answering this important question. There is a . . .

> living force that the message of Christ as "the resurrection and the life" set free among the early Christians, the force that enabled the new beginnings and the change that allowed men and women to create what had hitherto been unknown.... It holds within itself the fullness of life for which many people today are yearning.

> The modern world takes its bearings from humanistic and materialistic concepts of life. And what men and women experience there is a diminished life.... There is so much unlived, unloved, even sick life.... Believers, lovers, and the hopeful take their bearings from the living God and, in their closeness to God, experience life in its fullness.[2]

In this eloquent statement lie the key elements that bring hope to the church and world of today. Christian holiness is the *presence* of God's personal force for new beginnings in our lives, a grace-enabled *closeness* to God, life coming into its *fullness*. Going beyond being forgiven of sin, often called justification, holiness is more. It is becoming

---

1   Hubert P. Harriman and Barry L. Callen, *Color Me Holy: Holy God, Holy People* (Aldersgate Press, 2013), chaps. 4 and 5.

2   Jürgen Moltmann, *The Living God and the Fullness of Life* (Westminster John Knox Press, 2015), ix.

truly "alive to God in Christ Jesus" (Rom. 6:4-6, 11). It is a crucifixion of the old self that leads to this amazing result: "it is no longer I who live, but it is Christ who lives in me" (Gal. 2:20). Christ alive within is the holy life.[3]

This present book celebrates today's fresh movement of God through the holiness stream of the River of God. It is a contemporary flow of "the force," a resurgence of the "resurrection and the life" in Christ that originally launched the early church into the world. This resurgence can re-launch today's church into a world groping for meaning, cohesion, and even survival. The holy life in Christ's Spirit is a life with transcendence, life really alive within the fellowship of the Living God. It is life being experienced in its fullness by sheer grace.

> Christian holiness is the *presence* of God for new beginnings, for life coming into its *fullness*.

These pages focus on a particular network of church bodies that now are celebrating holiness and have chosen to comprise the WHC. It reviews the various dimensions of the holy stream represented within the traditions of this network. It spots and shares splashes of the River of God now moistening some of the most arid and troubling issues now before the faithful.

The WHC is a spontaneous network of Christian bodies anxious to share good news with hopeless, unsatisfied, and often socially irrelevant believers and congregations. These participating bodies realize that they can do this only because their very beings have been changed by the redeeming grace and abiding presence of God's Spirit. They have become committed to each other and to the enriching of the entire River of God. The richness comes from their closeness to God and the resulting fullness of life (holiness) that they are experiencing by God's unmerited grace. To God belongs all the glory!

---

3   See Barry L Callen, *Catch Your Breath!* (Aldersgate Press, 2014).

Springs Refreshing Today's Deserts

The ancient holiness stream of God's truth and pulsating life is newly rushing through the grace-full and life-giving River of God. What is ancient and biblical is also immediate and practical. This holiness-enriched River is one of "divine intimacy, a powerful river of holy living, a dancing river of jubilation in the Spirit, and a broad river of unconditional love for all peoples."[4]

The many writers found in these pages and their church affiliations have come to a common table, the Wesleyan Holiness Connection, with holiness central. They are sharing with each other their various currents of the rich holiness stream. They also are freshly addressing together the difficult issues through the lens of biblical holiness. Above all, they are networking and acting together to generate new life and mission relevance in today's Christian congregations worldwide.

> The WHC is a spontaneous network sharing good news for today's churches.

You are invited to join this movement of God. The Living God is offering fullness of life, new life for all peoples, and even for the earth itself. The following pages rejoice in the nourishing riches of the River of God flowing so freshly today. They glimpse the various facets of the holiness gem that have appeared in a range of centuries, denominations, and institutions of higher education. They also supply resources for engaging some of the most difficult issues facing the church and world today.

God indeed is on the move in our time. Join the rushing and cleansing waters coming from the very throne of God!

Barry L. Callen, Editor
Anderson, Indiana

---

4   Richard J. Foster, *Streams of Living Water: Celebrating the Great Traditions of Christian Faith* (HarperSanFrancisco, 1998), xv.

CONTRIBUTORS

Jim J. Adams

President of Life Pacific College, San Dimas, California

A. D. Beacham, Jr.

Presiding Bishop of the International Pentecostal Holiness Church

Robert Black

Professor of Religion, Southern Wesleyan University, and co-author of *The Story of The Wesleyan Church*

David Bundy

Research Professor for World Christian Studies, New York Theological Seminary; Honorary Fellow, Manchester Wesley Research Centre, Nazarene Theological College

Barry L. Callen

Dean Emeritus of Anderson University, longtime Editor of the *Wesleyan Theological Journal,* current Editor of Aldersgate Press and chair of its Publications Team, and member of the Board of Directors of the Wesleyan Holiness Connection

Brian Eckhardt

General Superintendent of the The Evangelical Church

James L. Edwards

President Emeritus of Anderson University, Anderson, Indiana

Sandra C. Gray

President of Asbury University, Wilmore, Kentucky

Hubert P. Harriman

President Emeritus of World Gospel Mission, Marion, Indiana

MaryAnn Hawkins

Dean, Director of the Doctor of Ministry Studies Program, Professor of Intercultural Studies, Anderson University School of Theology and Christian Ministry

Jack W. Hayford

Chancellor-Founder, The King's University, Southlake, Texas, and Pastor Emeritus, The Church On the Way, Van Nuys, California

Steve Hoskins

Ordained Elder of the Church of the Nazarene and Associate Professor of Religion, Trevecca Nazarene University, Nashville, Tennessee

Fawn Imboden

Director of Development, America's Christian Credit Union, Glendora, California, and staff support person for the Wesleyan Holiness Connection

Stan Ingersol

Nazarene Archives Manager, co-author of the centennial history of the Church of the Nazarene, and author of historical studies of the Holiness tradition

Jon Kulaga

Provost, Asbury University, Wilmore, Kentucky, and Publisher of Aldersgate Press of the Wesleyan Holiness Connection

Diane Leclerc

Professor of Historical Theology, Northwest Nazarene University, Nampa, Idaho

Jo Anne Lyon

General Superintendent Emerita of The Wesleyan Church, now serving as its Ambassador-at-Large, and founder of World Hope International

Kevin W. Mannoia

Founder and president of the Wesleyan Holiness Connection, Chaplain of Azusa Pacific University, former Bishop of the Free Methodist Church

Jose Ildo Swartele de Mello

Bishop of the Free Methodist Church, Brazil

Shirley A. Mullen

President of Houghton College, Houghton, New York

Kate Wallace Nunneley

Former Wesleyan Holiness Connection Operations Manager and co-founder of The Junia Project

Christopher D. O'Brien

Associate Pastor, Park Ridge Free Methodist Church, Rochester, New York, and Adjunct Professor, Fuller Theological Seminary

Kirsten Oh

Associate Professor of Practical Theology, Azusa Pacific University School of Theology, Elder in the California Pacific Annual Conference of the United Methodist Church

Clovis de Oliveira Paradela

Secretary of Planning and Projects, Methodist Region of Rio de Janeiro, Brazil, Wesleyan Holiness Connection Regional Coordinator for Rio de Janeiro State

John S. Pistole

President of Anderson University, Anderson, Indiana

Jonathan S. Raymond

President Emeritus of Trinity Western University & Seminary, Co-editor of *Word & Deed: The Salvation Army Journal of Theology and Ministry*

David G. Roebuck

Director, Dixon Pentecostal Research Center, and Assistant Professor of History and Church of God Historian, Lee University, Cleveland, Tennessee

Darrin J. Rodgers

Director of the Flower Pentecostal Heritage Center, Springfield, Missouri, and Editor of *Assemblies of God Heritage* magazine

E. Morris Sider

Professor Emeritus of History and English Literature, Messiah College, Mechanicsburg, Pennsylvania, former Editor of *Brethren in Christ History and Life*

Dan Schafer

President of World Gospel Mission and member of the Board of Directors of the Wesleyan Holiness Connection

Howard A. Snyder

Visiting Director, Manchester Wesley Research Centre, author of numerous books, including *Populist Saints: B. T. and Ellen Roberts and the First Free Methodists*

Henry Walter Spaulding II

President and Professor of Theology, Mount Vernon Nazarene University, Mount Vernon, Ohio

Sunberg, Carla

President and Professor of Historical Theology, Nazarene Theological Seminary, Kansas City, Missouri

Sunberg, Charles

Pastor, Church of the Nazarene, Coordinator of the WHC Regional Networks, and Member of the WHC Steering Committee

Joseph Tkach

President of Grace Communion International

Mendell L. Thompson

President and CEO, America's Christian Credit Union, Glendora, California

Don Thorsen

Professor of Theology and Director of the M. Div. program, Azusa Pacific University, and member of the Publications Team of Aldersgate Press

Bernie A. Van De Walle

Professor of Historical and Systematic Theology, M.Div. Program Advisor, Ambrose University, Calgary, Alberta, Canada

Kenneth L. Waters, Sr.

Associate Dean of the Division of Religion and Philosophy and Professor of New Testament, Azusa Pacific University, Azusa, California

Laurence W. Wood

The Frank Paul Morris Professor of Systematic Theology/Wesley Studies, Asbury Theological Seminary, Wilmore, Kentucky, and Founder/Publisher of Emeth Press, Lexington, Kentucky

THE
HOLY
RIVER
OF GOD

THE HOLY RIVER AND ITS STREAMS

The Holiness stream of Christianity runs wide and deep. It is full of life and inspires life wherever it goes. The holy God expects a holy people. This expectation is seen clearly throughout the Bible's revelation of God's working with fallen humanity.

The Spirit's work should result in a steady stream of purifying love with many currents that reflect both commonality and variety. Unfortunately, sometimes believers turn inward and build walls that become dams blocking the river's flow.

The central themes of the Holiness stream appear vividly in the thought of John Wesley. They also have appeared globally and in every century of church history. They particularly impacted North America in the nineteenth century and now offer fresh hope for the struggling Christian community of the twenty-first century.

Once realizing what God has provided and expects, believers "are discovering the moderating and multiplying power of weaving our lives together in unity" (Mannoia). Today's church needs "more women and men who really know a great God and are actively reflecting God's love in the world" (Callen/Waters).

CHAPTER 1

OUR GUIDING VISION FORWARD

by Kevin W. Mannoia

Picture in your mind's eye a vast expanse of desert. Then notice a river, a grand river that runs through it. This is the holy river of God's restorative mission in the world, principally represented by the work of the church. Amidst the dryness and human struggle for meaning, value, and wholeness, this river runs in stark contrast. Just like every river, this one is always moving; it is always changing; it is always life-giving.

Rivers are Alive and Bring Life

The holy river of God is always moving. It flows, sometimes with great speed and at other times with a meandering responsiveness to the contours of the landscape, but it is always moving forward inexorably in its ultimate purpose. If a river stops, it ceases to be a river and becomes something different – a lake, a pond. And with no movement, that water easily becomes a stagnant cesspool that attracts nothing but insects and odors.

A river is always changing. It is constantly carving its path through the world, responding to the ground and changing the landscape around it. Sometimes its course becomes straight and at other times it is winding. This river always seeks a path through the world as it moves in fulfillment of its purpose.

A river always brings life wherever it goes. When it flows into a body of water it keeps the water fresh and full of life. Where it flows, it magnetically draws people who choose to live along the river. It allows greenery, fruit, life, and hope to flourish. The river influences everything it touches, always bringing life.

The Holy River: One Source, Many Streams

As with any river, this holy river of God in the world has a source. It does not begin with councils, doctrine, or study. Nor does it begin in the ecclesiastical structures or actions of the institutional church, divine though they may be. It is not set in motion by fiat of a bishop or pastor. Nor does it spring up spontaneously where there are two or three Christians gathering together.

Rather, this grand river begins in the very heart of God, shaped and fueled by the nature of God. It is the best and most effective reflection of the character and passion of God in the desert of the world. God's holiness proceeding from love flavors and compels the flow of this river – moving, changing, and bringing life wherever it goes in the world.

This river has a purpose in the streets of broken cities, ivory towers of the academy, cubicles of everyday working people, and poor and affluent neighborhoods alike. It flows through sanctuaries and board rooms of churches, as well as executive suites around the world. There is no crevice of human life where this river may not have effect. The people of God who have chosen to leave the self-determination of the banks of the river and immerse themselves in the flow become the reflection of God in all the desert places of the world. Wherever we go, God's holy nature compelled by love is being reflected to the end that lives are restored, systems are redeemed, and all of creation is being made new.

> The holy river of God flows from the very heart of God.

In many ways this river of God is similar to any river we know. It has many streams or tributaries that flow into it, adding to its depth, breadth, and movement. Within each of those streams are currents that move, creating a robust diversity that reflects the wholeness of God's nature and life. These various streams are each unique. None is better than the others, but each is different. Some streams may flow rapidly through rocky terrain of conflict and struggle with white-water rapids. Others meander through meadows of cultural acceptance and integration in quiet peacefulness. Some have twists and curves responding to the events and changing human needs. Others are rather straight. Some run in the glare of the bright sun while others flow under the shade of canopied trees. Different, not better.

As we travel alongside the Holy River of God going upstream, we come to a number of these streams feeding the larger river. We come to one we might call the "Renewal in Mainline Denominations." Perhaps there is another stream called the "New Reformation Movement," and still another called the "Charismatic Catholic" stream. There are various such streams in the web of this great river system of God. Among these many streams of the church, we come to one that is called the "Wesleyan Holiness" stream.

The Wesleyan Holiness Stream

The Wesleyan Holiness stream of the church is rich with history, laden with serious thinking, and characterized by powerful manifestations of God's work in bringing change to culture in relevant and formative ways. Shaped by a deep Wesleyan theological framework, this stream leans into the mission of bringing the hope of God's salvation into the real circumstances of our lives. In seeking the essential unity of the church, the principles of integration, wholeness, curiosity, mission, and hospitality find their way relationally into the thinking patterns that inform Wesleyan-Holiness practice. The Wesleyan theological roots provide both an anchor to the historic church as well as a nimble practicality driven by a passion to bring the Kingdom of God into culture to make a difference now.

The Holiness identity in this stream is a spiritually vibrant manifestation of the Wesleyan theological framework in both personal transformation and social engagement, an expression of the otherness of God and the relevancy of the incarnation of Jesus. We are not set apart in exclusive isolation that devolves into legalism. Rather, while being transformed to reflect God's holiness, we engage in relevant incarnation and invite the world to join us in living in greater proximity to God who is holy. By reflecting God, we are compelled to engage in the real struggles of our culture. The people of this Wesleyan Holiness stream are on the forefront of championing the justice and love of God in practical and integrative ways.

Over the last two centuries, this Wesleyan Holiness stream of the church has taken the form of denominational families. Much like any family, these holiness denominations have found their individual distinctives in particular elements of the Wesleyan Holiness stream. In these particularities, they have brought to voice and clarity specific features that are central to their family stories. Each is an important aspect of the broader nature of God's holiness. In flowing together in this stream, these individual currents have created a fast-moving and fully-textured stream that pours healthy and authentic witness into the larger river of God.

As we explore these various currents within the Wesleyan Holiness stream, we find that our understanding of the depth, texture, and fullness of God's holiness is beyond what any one of our denominational families can represent individually. In fact, we really do need each other. We are not diffused by these differing traits, but rather deepened as we weave our currents together and thereby discover a fuller vision of God's holiness and motivating love. Pastors and leaders begin to realize that the holiness of God is broader than they thought when viewing it simply from their own family perspective.[1]

---

1   A fuller discussion of the effects of diverse perspectives on the kingdom of heaven may be found in the chapter "The Stargate Effect" in Kevin W. Mannoia, *Church 2K: Leading Forward* (Precedent Press, 2007).

Seeing through the eyes of others allows us to gain new perspectives on God's fuller nature. The result is that we all are made better for it. Appreciation for our own family current is deepened and we are better able to both learn and contribute to the diverse unity of the church. As I often tell pastors in the many events of the Wesleyan Holiness Connection, "We are not diminishing your leader's commitment to his or her denomination, but rather enhancing their commitment to their own particular family as they come to know better the fullness of God's holiness through the eyes of others in their stream."

Unfortunate Sojourn into Legalism

In the history of the Wesleyan Holiness movement, typical patterns of organizational development over generations have caused the churches to become distracted and somewhat misguided. The denominational families in the Holiness movement were founded by people full of passion and fire as they were consumed by God's Spirit. As they allowed that inner fire to compel them, behaviors changed and fresh initiatives made a difference in the cultural issues of their day. For example, the Booths were compelled by an inner fire to reach to the streets of London; Roberts, Scott, and others were driven by the passion for the holy to engage the political and cultural issues of slavery; Bresee, Warner, Palmer, McPherson, and others were consumed by the need for wholeness arising from inner piety and full salvation.

As the next generation began to pick up the mantle, they saw the powerful work of God through their predecessors and sought to continue it through new programs and behaviors. But this generation tended to focus on the behaviors and structures themselves, thereby beginning the process of codifying particularities of the movement into institutional behaviors. Ultimately, these distinctive behaviors turned into denominational regulations that became imposed on members as a necessary sign of true loyalty. This tendency toward equating vibrancy in holiness with institutional compliance was the beginning of a heavy yoke of legalism which most denominations struggled with for decades.

Whether in the Pentecostal or Revivalist currents of the Holiness movement, particular points of behavioral traits became restrictive litmus tests of the depth of commitment and true reflection of God's holiness. This legalism lured most denominational families into impotency. Many churches sought to build their denominational reach and influence through institutional structures. This institutional emphasis created unfortunate walls of division.

In an effort to codify family distinctives, institutions and structures were formed as the focus of mission. They turned into walls built within the holiness stream. As they became increasingly self-perpetuating and institutionally focused, they got out of alignment with the missional flow of the stream. They became almost synonymous with the very mission of each church. In effect, these rose higher in importance than the water level of the missional stream. Institutional outcomes drove the efforts. Of course, once a wall becomes higher than the flow of the river, it ceases to be a channel and becomes a dam.

This damming of the flow of the Wesleyan Holiness stream of the church became so intense as to cause many to see these "holiness" people and churches as legalistic, restrictive fundamentalists. Many abandoned the very word "holiness" as pejorative. Generations left the churches of their parents in an effort to escape the oppressive environments. Because of the perception that holiness people were exclusive and legalistic, even its own leaders shied away from self-identification with holiness. Some even said that the holiness movement was dead.

The Holiness Movement Is Alive!

Thankfully God's flow of holiness in the world is not silenced by the harm we perpetrate on it in our efforts to control and define it. With shrinking impact and loss of identity, some within this stream began to seek the holy fire of God again. The holiness message has become a unifying center to the church families birthed in that distinct stream of the church. Whether Pentecostal or Revivalist, we are discovering the moderating effect and multiplying power of weaving our lives together in unity. The differing currents of the Holiness stream are flavoring each other with a richness that is bringing into synergy and greater focus the missional nature of holiness in the twenty-first century.[2] By God's grace, a signifi-cant center of this synergy and flavoring is happen-ing through the networks of the Wesleyan Holiness Connection (see particularly chapters 21-29 of this volume).

> The walls that became dams are being realigned into channels for God's holiness to flow freely.

The walls that became dams are being readjusted and realigned to become again the channels of God's holiness in the world, encouraging fast-moving, fresh water to rush into the larger river of God. These walls are not being destroyed but are becoming permeable. They remain as a helpful narrative to the unique family stories of many denominations within this stream (many are found elsewhere in this book). Much like picket fences, they encourage a permeable interaction among the various family currents enabling both celebration of the unique family stories and collaboration in lifting the holiness of God as a transform-ing message of unity.

---

2   The concept of synergy through unity is explained further in an article titled "The Diversity of Unity" by Kevin W. Mannoia and T. D. Jakes in *Charisma* (Fall, 2001).

CHAPTER 2

THE HOLINESS STREAM IN BIBLICAL AND HISTORICAL CONTEXT

by Barry L. Callen and Kenneth L. Waters, Sr.

"Holiness"? It's a quintessential attribute of God. The core meaning is separateness from all that is evil, unclean, and ordinary. Therefore, holiness points toward all that transcends the finiteness of this passing world. For us humans, holiness is being separate from evil, cleansed from fallenness, elevated to true Christ-likeness, finding a oneness with the life of God.

A lofty goal? Yes, of course, but addressing seriously the subject of holiness from a biblical point of view leads this way. The subject is not the mere preoccupation of emotional revivalists, religious individualists, or narrow-minded legalists. It's the heart of biblical revelation and thus essential for disciples of Jesus who desire to be God's faithful and effective people in this world.

Christian holiness is intended by God to be universal in scope and missionary in nature. The point is *participation*. God wants all people to be in renewed relationship with the divine and then active citizens of a holy church for the sake of the salvation of a lost world. Those committed to holiness are to conduct themselves in a way that commends faith in the Holy One. The point is to encourage others to see a real-life difference in Christian believers and be drawn to God's holy grace that alone makes such difference possible.

First Peter 2:12 makes clear the task of proper Christian living: "Conduct yourselves honorably among the Gentiles so that, though they malign you as evildoers, they may see your honorable deeds and glorify God when he comes to judge."

Periodic renewal of a holiness emphasis has been the goal of numerous Christian movements over the centuries. Doctrinal apostasy, excessive church institutionalization, and/or compromise with prevailing cultures have plagued the Jesus people. In response, reform movements have sought to reverse such negative trends. They have brought back honorable conduct that glorifies God by reflecting in this world the will and ways of God.

> Just as God is holy, so the people of God are to be holy.

Such holiness reformers have influenced the established churches either by renewing them or moving beyond them when necessary. Given the Bible's strong concern for holiness of heart and life,[1] holiness should be appreciated for its rich past and its potential for meeting the great spiritual and social needs of the present.

Biblical Foundations

Directly or indirectly, the entire Bible addresses the subject of holiness. Basic to all of its witness is the revealed fact that God is holy. Isaiah 6 begins with the seraphs crying out to one another: "Holy, holy, holy is the Lord of hosts; the whole earth is full of his glory." This is the holy God of biblical revelation.

We then are told something startling and most demanding. Just as God is holy, so *the people of God are to be holy*: "Like obedient children, do not be conformed to the desires that you formerly had in ignorance. Instead, as he who called you is holy, be holy yourselves in all your

---

1   See Barry L. Callen and Don Thorsen, eds., *Heart & Life: Rediscovering Holy Living* (Aldersgate Press, 2012).

conduct; for it is written, 'You shall be holy, for I am holy'" (1 Peter 1:14-16).

The entire biblical narrative is about holiness granted, lost, and recovered. This long biblical journey toward a renewed holiness started with a creation in perfect relation to God, a circumstance that tragically changed by human choice. The struggle was then on for the elect people of God to be cleansed again and made a whole (holy) people in relation to a holy God and in the midst of a fallen world. God called people to be filled with his Spirit, to be his very own, to be like him, to be an instrument of holiness restoration, a truly set-apart people bringing light to the nations.

Biblically speaking, the ultimate goal of a believer's spiritual life is to be holy – separate from the world, cleansed from sin, elevated to Christ-likeness in being and action, and an active member of a holy people, the church on mission. Holiness is defined by the very nature of God as that is understood best in Jesus Christ.

Holiness is not restricted to spiritual elites, believers who are especially emotional or those who hope to escape this world by being radically different and safely disconnected. To the contrary, holiness is for all who believe in the biblical God made known through Jesus Christ. It is for all who believe and are willing to be submissive to God's Spirit and part of what God intends, the redemption of this present world.

Unfortunately, so the biblical story goes, this liberated people of God chose to be "like the nations," unholy, living by their own values and self-reliance, not by God's grace and law. The people decided to do their own thing like everybody else. By being like the nations in attitudes, social practices, and even political organization and military reliance, God's people chose to be unlike God, thus unholy and not available for God's mission. The result was disaster (Ezek. 5:5-12).

The biblical prophets repeatedly make clear that a lack of holiness is evidenced in three ways by those supposed to be God's own people: (1) there is social injustice quietly sanctioned; (2) there is inordinate trust in the sword – their own money, traditions, talents, and influence; and (3) the people hide behind a life of false worship in which God takes no delight, no matter how good it looks, sounds, or even smells (Amos 5:21).

The earliest Christian movement was successful in its expansion and dramatic influence primarily because the risen Christ pulsated with divine life within and among the believers. They chose holiness, living "in him" (Col. 2:16). Being the holy people of God did not center in formulas of spiritual experience or codebooks of precise dos and don'ts. Instead, it centered in the Spirit of God being present and active through willing hearts. Nothing is more likely to draw the unbelieving nations to God than openly living lives that look like Jesus and are empowered by the Spirit of Jesus.

The goal of the Christian spiritual pilgrimage was then and still should be having the mind that was in Christ Jesus (Phil. 2:1-11). Sharing that mind through the wisdom, gifting, and empowerment of God's Spirit is being holy.

Holiness Traditions in Church History

The Roman Catholic Church has had a long and influential emphasis on Christian holiness, beginning with its monastic tradition. Franciscans and Dominicans emphasize holiness through mendicant vows. Carmelites emphasize holiness through contemplative prayer, while Jesuits do it more through missionary and educational work. This multi-dimensioned holiness stream has been brought into the present by Pope Francis and his 2013 apostolic exhortation titled *The Joy of the Gospel*. Francis calls believers to a renewed personal encounter with Jesus Christ so that we might be drawn out of ourselves – our fears, weaknesses, sins, and self-centeredness – and brought into the fullness of life found only with living *in* God and *for* others.[2]

---

2   See Edward Sri, *Rediscovering the Heart of a Disciple: Pope Francis and "The Joy of the Gospel"* (Our Sunday Visitor, Inc., 2014).

The ancient Orthodox Church represents a long tradition of under-lining the Christian's need for holiness as a *living spiritual experience.* Being faithful to Christ is not seen as primarily the acceptance of a set of creedal texts or worship customs inherited from past generations, but rather the personal and direct experience of the Holy Spirit in the present. The "mystical" tradition of Christianity also affirms such di-rect spiritual immediacy and life transformation as holiness essentials. Before the *doing* must come the *being.*

The Anabaptist or "Radical" Christian tradition joins this holiness stream with certain variations. It sees the church being in the world in a distinctive holy and cross – like way. This Jesus way is marked by grace, life in the Spirit, and living in a disciplined church community marked by commitments to peace and self-giv-ing servanthood. Holiness is defined in this way: "The church serves best the gospel of Christ and a lost world when it derives its life and legitimacy, its vision and standards, from the Christian gospel. The church becomes good news for the world only when its own unique existence emerges from the gospel and becomes the Christ community living visibly in and for the world."[3]

> Holiness is about forming communities that reflect the Spirit of Christ in today's world.

The goal of being truly "in Christ" or "going on to perfection" (holiness) is a persistent and prominent concern in the Bible and among the followers of Jesus who have hoped to be the disciples that Jesus desires and enables. Becoming a new creation in Christ is a reality available to every believer in this life by way of the sanctify-ing grace of God. So says the Bible and spiritually sensitive believers who have lived across the centuries and been affiliated with multiple church traditions.

---

3   See Howard A. Snyder, *The Radical Wesley* (Seedbed, rev. ed., 2014), and Barry L. Callen, *Radical Christianity: Believers Church Tradition in Christianity's History and Future* (Evangel Publishing House, 1999), 123.

This holiness tradition greatly impacted the social and religious landscape of Great Britain in the eighteenth century, especially through the ministries of John and Charles Wesley. They came to embody key elements of the ancient Orthodox and more recent mystical, Roman Catholic, and Protestant holiness traditions. The goal was not to create a new church body or the building of a new theological system. Rather, it was to reintroduce an "optimism of grace" that can transform lives into holy and responsible agents of divine love.[4]

The holiness movement of the nineteenth century in the United States helped make possible the rise of Pentecostalism in the early twentieth century. This was a fresh search for a fuller integrity of life in God's Spirit, the ongoing search for a credible Christian holiness that truly transforms lives and advances the kingdom of God on earth.

We now are in the early twenty-first century with all its violence and change. The spiritual need is great, as is the need for authentic Christian disciples who obviously have been with Jesus and are willing to be with the world as Jesus was. It may be that the church is beginning to experience what the earliest church did, *an age of the Spirit*. The Wesleyan Holiness Connection believes this to be the case and is seeking to be a catalyst for the emergence of such a wonderful reality.

Holiness in the Wesleyan tradition is hardly something new. It is biblically rooted and has always been flowing from the heart of God into the hearts of receptive disciples. By God's grace and the faithfulness of God's people, the Holy River of God soon will be at flood stage!

Reflecting a Great God

Holiness is about life being transformed by God's Spirit. It is about serious believers in Jesus Christ seeking to be, by the grace of God, who they are intended to be. It is about forming communities of faith that

---

4   See Randy L. Maddox, *Responsible Grace: John Wesley's Practical Theology* (Kingswood Books, 1994).

reflect the Spirit of Christ by actively being about Christ's agenda in today's world, an agenda of unity, justice, love, and peace.

It has been said that Western culture may be nearing a point at which the Christian faith can be successfully reintroduced. If there is a pending collapse of the present order of things, nothing can credibly replace the emptiness except an outbreak of revolutionary, holiness-oriented faith in Jesus Christ and the love flowing from him. May it be so!

Biblical revelation and church history make one thing very clear. God still wants a people who will dare to be his own. We are to love and trust God and risk being like God in character and with God redemptively in divine mission.

Today's church does not need more "great" women and men of God. It needs more women and men who really know a great God, and in that relationship of knowing are actively reflecting God's love to the world. As Jesus once said, we become truly holy when we humbly and gratefully pray, "Hallowed be God's name."[5]

---

5   See Barry L. Callen, *The Prayer of Holiness-Hungry People: A Disciple's Guide to the Lord's Prayer* (Francis Asbury Press, 2011).

CHAPTER 3

JOHN WESLEY'S HOLINESS THEMES

by Don Thorsen and Kirsten Oh

John Wesley was the spiritual and theological inspiration for the modern Holiness tradition of Protestant Christianity. He led a great revival in eighteenth-century England, and he – along with his brother Charles – founded the Methodist movement. The influence of Methodism spread to the United States, stimulating the development of the Holiness tradition of churches and denominations dedicated to proclaiming and living holiness for the benefit of individuals and societies as a whole.

Although many factors contributed to Wesley's understanding of holy living, the following eight themes are crucial. They help us understand the importance of biblical holiness, how it spawned the development of the modern Holiness tradition, and how it may be effectively preached, taught, and practiced in the complex, diverse, and global context in which we live today.

1. God Is Love

Scripture describes God both as holy and as love, and it was important for John Wesley to think about holiness in terms of love (Isaiah 6:3; 1 John 4:8). There are many attributes that Scripture ascribes to God: sovereignty, creativity, eternity, and more. Many Christians think of God first as sovereign and powerful, and Wesley affirmed such attributes. However, he considered it important to think more about God as holy, loving, and relational.

God made provision for reconciliation through the atonement of Jesus Christ. Although people's choices are enabled by God's grace, they represent genuine choices that people are to make, accepting or rejecting God's offer of salvation. So our relationship with God should be understood primarily as a love relationship that is holy, and not primarily as a relationship based on sovereignty and power. Wesley's emphasis on God as holy and loving influenced the Holiness tradition's proclamation of the God who loves and seeks by the Holy Spirit to become reconciled with people by means of the gospel of Jesus Christ.

2. Primacy of Scripture

Wesley never tired of reading, studying, and proclaiming Scripture. He famously described himself as *homo unius libri* (Latin, "a man of one book").[1] For Wesley, Scripture was the divine revelation of God, inspired by the Holy Spirit, and sufficient for all matters of Christian faith and practice.

Wesley emphasized the primacy of biblical authority. He also talked about the genuine – albeit secondary – religious authorities of church tradition, critical thinking, and relevant experience. Later referred to as the "Wesleyan quadrilateral," Wesley's emphasis on Scripture, tradition, reason, and experience enabled him to present a dynamic way of understanding and promoting the full gospel of Jesus Christ.[2] It was a gospel that affects more than people's beliefs and values; it also impacts their lives, day-to-day practices, and ministries.

---

1   John Wesley, Preface (1746), *Sermons on Several Occasions*, §5, in *The Works of John Wesley*, ed. Albert C. Outler (Nashville: Abingdon Press, 1984), 1.105.

2   Don Thorsen, *The Wesleyan Quadrilateral: Scripture, Tradition, Reason and Experience as a Model of Evangelical Theology* (1990 rpt.; Lexington, KY: Emeth Press, 2005), 5-7.

3. Unholy Sin

Wesley was concerned about the state of humanity, of those who are separated from God because of their sin, their unholy rejection of God which results in death, judgment, and the corruption of their lives – individually and socially, spiritually and physically. All are sinful; all are in need in God's grace for their salvation and restoration of the image of God in which they were created (Gen. 1:26-27). However, people are not without hope.

From Wesley's perspective, the majority of Christians in church history affirmed people's responsibility for their sin and their faith and repentance. God partners with people, enabling them to choose to respond to God's offer of salvation. This partnering continues beyond conversion. God wants believers to grow in grace, opening themselves to the leading and empowerment of the Holy Spirit, leading to greater Christ-

> Salvation is a single and complex reality full of eternal destiny.

likeness, love, and holiness. In so doing, Wesley argued that people increasingly can overcome sin in their lives. Although they may not become absolutely perfect, God provides grace to aid in overcoming trials and temptations.

4. Soteriological Focus

Although Wesley is often remembered as a champion of holiness, the salvation of people was his highest priority in ministry. His focus upon salvation – soteriological focus – appears in the very first of his published sermons: "Salvation by Faith." He followed the Protestant emphasis on the need for people to respond to God's calling with conversion, by faith and repentance. But salvation does not end with conversion; it represents the beginning of God's reconciling and restorative process.

For Wesley, salvation was a single, complex event, which lasted throughout the lives of believers. Although they may convert in a moment, there is no single timing for being saved. Salvation occurs as a kind of therapeutic restoration, not in a psychological sense, but in a holistic sense of healing all of people's lives. Randy Maddox says: "Wesley characterized the very essence of religion as . . . a therapy by which the Great Physician heals our sin-diseased souls, restoring the vitality of life that God intended for us."[3]

5. Entire Sanctification

Perhaps the most distinctive aspect of Wesley's emphasis on holiness had to do with his affirmation of entire sanctification. He took seriously biblical claims to be holy, to be entirely sanctified. For example, Paul said: "May the God of peace himself sanctify you entirely; and may your spirit and soul and body be kept sound and blameless at the coming of our Lord Jesus Christ" (1 Thess. 5:23). Rather than interpret these biblical passages as symbolic, or as unachievable goals, Wesley believed that Christians should take them seriously.

The Christian "perfection" or entire sanctification, to which God leads us is towards love: loving God with our whole heart, soul, mind, and strength, and loving our neighbors as we love ourselves (Mark 12:28-31).[4] The heart of holiness is love toward God, neighbor, and ourselves. We may fall short in our performance of love, but Wesley thought that believers could reach a point of intentionality in always doing that which is loving. Usually this heightened sense of consecration to the Lordship of Jesus Christ occurs subsequent to conversion, perhaps as a second crisis of decision. At the point when we as believers realize that Jesus wants to be more than our Savior, we are to offer ourselves as a "living sacrifice, holy and acceptable," which God empowers graciously for our entire sanctification (Rom. 12:1).

---

3   Randy L. Maddox, *Responsible Grace: John Wesley's Practical Theology* (Nashville: Kingswood Books), 145.

4   John Wesley, *A Plain Account of Christian Perfection, as Believed and Taught by the Reverend Mr. John Wesley from the Year 1725 to the Year 1777.* Reprinted (Kansas City: Beacon Hill Press, 1966), 14, 99, 119.

Wesley was not always as clear as we would like with regard to the timing and degree of holiness that we may achieve in this present life. As a result, some in the Holiness tradition have emphasized degrees of perfectionism and of the eradication of sin that far surpasses Wesley's articulated understanding of entire sanctification. Be that as it may, Wesley remained hopeful – as should we – about how God wants us to go on to holiness, to living more and more like Jesus, and in loving God and our neighbors as ourselves.

6. No Holiness but Social Holiness

Wesley's statement that there is "no holiness but social holiness" emphasizes how growth in Christ-likeness occurs best when it occurs in accountability with other Christians.[5] Sometimes the phrase is mistakenly used to describe Wesley's social consciousness and advocacy on behalf of those who are poor. Although he was socially active, social holiness had to do with the various means of grace described in Scripture by which believers may grow spiritually in relationship with others.

> Christians are to engage in compassionate ministries on behalf of the impoverished and unjustly treated.

Christian "conferencing" emphasizes how believers should hold one another accountable, helping to facilitate each other's growth in grace. Wesley was a master organizer – a methodical leader – who created mid-week small groups called Societies. For those who wanted more intimacy and accountability, groups met in "class meetings" in which members held one another spiritually accountable. For those who most wanted to go on to holiness, smaller groups were created called "bands." Such dedication continued in the development of the Holiness tradition, facilitating its growth in ways similar to early Methodism.

---

5   John Wesley, Preface, *Hymns and Sacred Poems* (1739), in *The Works of John Wesley*, 3rd ed., ed. Thomas Jackson (Grand Rapids: Baker Book House, 1978), 14.321.

7. Empowering Ministries

Wesley was a pioneer in empowering new and contextually appropriate ministries that continue to inspire members of the Wesleyan, Methodist, Pentecostal, and Holiness traditions. Although he sometimes balked at being innovative, and some Anglican leaders persecuted him for it, Wesley did not cease pursuing the best ways of ministering to others. For example, he practiced open-air preaching and evangelism, especially among those who were poor.

Women were empowered by Wesley, first to serve as lay leaders among women, and later among men as well. Both biblically and experientially, he recognized the authentic ministries that women performed, and so Wesley permitted them to teach and preach. He pioneered an egalitarian view of women in ministry, and his role model influenced the early development in the Holiness tradition. For example, B. T. Roberts, founding Bishop of the Free Methodist Church, wrote *Ordaining Women* (1891). Women in the Salvation Army received the same officer privileges as their husbands, sharing in one another's ministries.

8. Compassion and Advocacy

Christians and churches have historically engaged in compassion ministries on behalf of those who are impoverished, uneducated, and unjustly treated. Wesley ministered through works of mercy on behalf of "the least of these" in society (Matt. 25:40, 45); such works exemplify holiness in action. But he did more. Wesley advocated on behalf of changing slave laws that were too lax and perpetuated violence as well as unjust treatment of Africans captured as slaves. Wesley's last known letter (1791) was to William Wilberforce, a champion of abolitionism in the British Parliament.

During the nineteenth century, Christians and churches in the Holiness tradition were leaders in advocating on behalf of social injustices caused by the marginalization of people and their oppressive treatment. For example, the Wesleyan Methodist Church came into existence advocating for the abolition of slavery. The Free Methodist Church also advocated abolitionism, along with free pews so that the poor were not relegated to the worst seats in a church. The Salvation Army championed ministries to the poor.

Conclusion

These eight themes represent ways that John Wesley influenced the development and continuation of the Holiness tradition of Christianity. That tradition includes most believers who consider themselves to be Wesleyan, Methodist, Holiness, or Pentecostal Christians. Thus, he continues to be a standard bearer for all today who wish to experience and promote biblical holiness, manifested primarily as love – love for God and for one's neighbor.

CHAPTER 4

THE INTERNATIONAL HOLINESS AND PENTECOSTAL MOVEMENTS

by David Bundy

The Holiness and Pentecostal movements around the world comprise about 500 million adherents of Christianity. These movements are generally divided into small denominations or units. They range in size from single small congregations to the Salvation Army with its nearly six million members/adherents or the Church of God in Christ and several Latin American and African churches which are probably larger.

Theologically these groups are diverse and always evolving as they seek to explain their faith in a quite complicated world. They include churches that often emphasize their Methodist identity, but sometimes also their Quaker, Lutheran, Brethren, Reformed, Congregationalist, Unitarian, Anglican, Presbyterian, Anabaptist, Orthodox, Church of God, and Baptist heritages. Some identify as "Pentecostal" and some as 'Sanctified" churches.

Seeking Holiness

The Holiness and Pentecostal movements around the world, with their many diversities, depend to a certain extent on theological decisions made by the Moravians, Zinzendorf, and the late nineteenth-century

Holiness movements.[1] The Holiness and/or Pentecostal movements on any given continent have never been united into a single organization; most are not well acquainted with the wide range of the related movements around the world.

> Holiness groups are diverse and have numerous heritages.

Most countries have churches that do or could trace their heritages back to the Moravians, Quakers, John Wesley, William Taylor, J. C. Blumhardt, Phoebe Palmer, William and Catharine Booth, Richard Reader Harris, Mary Baxter, Andrew Murray, C. P. Jones, V. A. Pashkov, Martin Wells Knapp, John Sung, or William Seymour.

Holiness teaching has always been controversial. In the Roman Catholic Church, those who promoted holiness were isolated in orders or in quasi orders such as the Brethren of the Common Life or the Cathari who were eradicated. In Protestantism, the phobia of "works" among Lutherans and groups influenced by them led to persecution or isolation of groups that emphasized holiness in this life. Thus, the Pietists and later the Moravians were considered almost heretics by both Lutherans and Catholics. They said, in effect, "How dare one argue that Christians can be better Christians if they actively strive to love God wholeheartedly and their neighbors as themselves!" For holiness people, personal consecration and social ministry were considered inseparable aspects of the "Great Commandment."

In England and its colonies that became the United States, versions of Methodism and the holiness movements developed under the leadership of Methodists such as Lorenzo Dow, Richard Allen, Francis Asbury, Timothy Merritt, and the Palmers, but also among Presbyterians such as Asa Mahan and Charles Finney of Oberlin College.[2] The work

---

1   W. R. Ward, *Global Evangelicalism: A Global Intellectual History, 1670-1789* (Cambridge: Cambridge University Press, 2006).

2   Nathan O. Hatch, *The Democratization of American Christianity* (New Haven: Yale University Press, 1989).

of William E. Boardman, *The Higher Christian Life* (copyright 1859), brought the Holiness Movement to Presbyterians, Anglicans, Brethren, and to many Methodists. It was translated, in whole or in part, into most Western European languages. Boardman also organized, with Robert Pearsall Smith and Hannah Whitall Smith, internationally important conferences on holiness at Oxford and Brighton.[3]

From 1874, the interdenominational international Holiness Movement was known as the "Oxford Movement." It became influential in Britain, France, Germany, Sweden, Russia, and a host of other countries. Normally it promoted evangelism, sanctification, ministry of women, deaconess work, prison ministry, missions, and healing. Outside of Germany and France, there were many women in leadership, including as preachers and teachers. Ecclesiological definition depended on the individual and context.[4]

In North America, the Methodist Holiness movements fragmented, often separating from the Methodist churches. Those who became more ecumenical, insisting that the Baptism of the Holy Spirit could overcome the divisions between Christians, and who were willing to revise traditional Methodist theology to insist upon healing and premillennial eschatology, became the Radical Holiness Movement. "Baptism with the Holy Spirit," with the use of the biblical Pentecost narratives and reading the Bible with those narratives as the primary interpretative focus, became central.

The Radical Holiness Movement men and women spread (c. 1880-1920) Radical Holiness around the world, making common cause with non-Methodist and sometimes Methodist expressions of the 1870 holiness revivals. This produced independent groups, later denominations, in Europe, Asia, and Africa. In the USA, between 1895 and 1920,

---

3   Melvin E. Dieter, *The Holiness Revival of the Nineteenth Century* (2nd ed., Lanham: Scarecrow Press, 1996).

4   David Bundy, *Visions of Apostolic Mission: Scandinavian Pentecostal Mission to 1935* (Studia Historico-ecclesiastica Upsaliensia, 45; Uppsala: Uppsala University, 2009).

groups as diverse as the Metropolitan Church Association, Church of the Nazarene, Pilgrim Holiness Church, Pentecostal Holiness Church, the Assemblies of God, and many others brought together Radical Holiness individuals and groups for cooperative ministry and mission. These often called themselves "Pentecostal."[5]

Holiness Seeking Unity

During the early years of the twentieth century, as Radical Holiness groups around the world were coalescing. Some chose to identify themselves as Pentecostals, with heightened emphasis on glossolalia, prophecy, and healing as important liturgical and praxis foci. The new Pentecostal movements spread across the world, inspired by the thought of William Seymour in Los Angeles, who connected "Baptism with the Holy Spirit" as evidenced by glossolalia and other spiritual gifts with power for effective mission. Most of the early leaders of the Pentecostal movements were to varying degrees associated with the Radical Holiness movements around the world. The newer radicals shared common heroes (such as William Taylor and Pandita Ramabai) and common theological motifs with the previous generation.[6]

"Holiness and Unity" has become an international forum for Holiness and Pentecostal churches.

During the second quarter of the twentieth century in North America, Holiness and Pentecostal denominations were invited to

---

5 Vinson Synan, *The Holiness Pentecostal Movement in the United States* (Grand Rapids: William B. Eerdmans Publishing Company, 1971); William Kostlevy, *Holy Jumpers: Evangelicals and Radicals in Progressive Era America* (Oxford: Oxford University Press, 2010); and Mary Lou Shea, *I Need Your Prayers and Patience: The Life and Ministry of Hiram F. Reynolds* (Eugene: Wipf & Stock/Resource Publications, 2015).

6 Allan Anderson, *An Introduction to Pentecostalism: Global Charismatic Christianity* (Cambridge; New York: Cambridge University Press, 2004); and David Bundy, *Visions of Apostolic Mission: Scandinavian Pentecostal Mission to 1935* (Uppsala University Library, 2009).

enter ecumenical movements such as the National Association of Evangelicals, often at the cost of changing their doctrinal statements or de-emphasizing holiness and pentecostal ideals of personal holiness and social ministry and the distinctive Pentecostal spirituality practices. Because of theological strife and competition, Holiness and Pentecostal churches became estranged. They built separate ecumenical groups: the National Holiness Association (later Christian Holiness Association and then Christian Holiness Partnership [CHP]), and the Pentecostal Fellowship of North America which was dissolved in 1994 to create the Pentecostal/Charismatic Churches of North America (PCCNA). The CHP dissolved in 2002.

"Holiness and Unity" has become a new international forum for both Holiness and Pentecostal churches to emphasize personal and social holiness, while allowing the denominations to follow their own cultural and denominational evolutions. The Wesleyan Holiness Connection originating in North America is a prime example – its web address is *holinessandunity.org*. Other Holiness and Pentecostal ecumenical projects are being undertaken in Asia, Europe, Australia, and Africa.

CHAPTER 5

THE AMERICAN HOLINESS MOVEMENT

by Stan Ingersol

A merica proved to be ground where a nation of immigrants and dissenters could experiment boldly with change. Social, political, and religious landscapes were altered repeatedly. From this ferment, and with an air of insurgency, the American Holiness Movement emerged in the nineteenth century.

A Religion of the Heart

The call to holiness is embedded in the Old and New Testaments. Christians have responded to it variously, from the solitary monasticism of the early desert Fathers to the communal monasticism of medieval and modern eras. John Wesley insisted that this call addresses every Christian regardless of station or vocation. Sanctification constituted "a main thread throughout [his] sermons, determining both the shape of his theology and the tone of his preaching."[1]

Wesley embraced "the religion of the heart," a Protestant style emphasizing religious experience. Pietists, as they were called, had a distinctive vocabulary and conversed earnestly about justification, sanctification, and Christian assurance. They gathered for intimate

---

1   Richard P. Heitzenrater, ed., *The Elusive Mr. Wesley*, 2 vols. (Nashville: Abingdon Press, 1984), 1:151.

spiritual conversation. Wesley met Lutheran and Moravian Pietists on two continents, absorbed some of their spiritual style, and adapted their methods. Guided by his vision, Methodists gathered thousands into classes and bands where holy living was facilitated through self-examination, testimony, confession, and the practice of spiritual disciplines.

A trans-denominational holiness movement flowed from four primary channels beginning in the 1830s.

After English and Irish immigrants brought Methodism to America, the American Holiness Movement emerged in the 1830s. Several generations of camp meeting and revival preachers had pursued the conversion of sinners, but holiness preachers used revivals and camp meetings to bring Christian believers into "the deeper experience" of "entire sanctification." They created their own literature and publishing companies and conducted their own holiness camp meetings and conventions.

All of this activity became a trans-denominational holiness movement that eventually flowed down four primary channels. Two of these developed in the 1830s – a Wesleyan-holiness movement tied to Methodism and an Oberlin holiness movement largely among Congregationalists and Presbyterians.

The Wesleyan-Holiness Movement

In 1836, sisters Sarah Lankford and Phoebe Palmer gathered Methodist women from two New York City churches and formed the Tuesday Meeting for the Promotion of Holiness. Men eventually joined the circle. Those frequently in attendance later included Methodist bishops and Rev. Nathan Bangs, head of Methodist publishing.

Meanwhile, Rev. Timothy Merritt of New England published *The Christian's Manual* (1824), a book explicitly advocating the entire sanctification of believers. In 1839 he initiated *The Guide to Christian Perfection*, a monthly journal that published testimonies and publicized the activities of the Tuesday Meeting and similar circles of spiritual life. As this revival movement expanded among Methodists, it also gained adherents in other denominations.

Palmer began traveling as a lay speaker and theologian. Her writings included treatises on Christian perfection, such as *The Way of Holiness* (1843), but her most distinctive contribution may have been *Promise of the Father* (1859), a theology establishing a biblical basis for women's preaching.

After the Civil War, the movement shifted to a new phase. In 1867 a group of Methodist ministers summoned nearly twenty thousand to a great national camp meeting in Vineland, New Jersey. A new organization formed to sustain the momentum. Known popularly as the National Holiness Association, it sponsored national camp meetings annually and inspired the formation of dozens of state and local holiness associations.

The Wesleyan-Holiness movement also found constituents in churches that had not stemmed from Methodism, including Quakers and various Anabaptist and Church of God circles.

Oberlin Holiness

Charles Finney's towering personality stood behind the Oberlin holiness movement, which also emerged in the 1830s. After a dramatic conversion experience, Finney entered the ministry and became a successful revivalist, but he grew disappointed with converts who backslid. This led him to emphasize a "second work of grace" that would ground them more firmly in the faith. He joined the faculty of Oberlin College in Ohio as professor of theology and later served as president.

Asa Mahan participated with Finney in developing Oberlin's brand of holiness theology, which emphasized a complete consecration of the human will to God. Oberlin theology produced no new denominations, with the college as its primary institutional achievement, influencing Presbyterians and Congregationalists for nearly two generations. Its greater impact was on American society, as it stoked the flames of abolitionism and the empowerment of women. Antoinette Brown, the first American woman ordained to the ministry, was an Oberlin graduate.

Keswick Holiness

A third stream of holiness revivalism developed back in England. There were American influences. Finney preached across England twice in the 1850s, and Phoebe Palmer spent four years in Christian service there. In the 1870s, Quaker holiness evangelists Hannah and Pearsall Smith conducted holiness meetings in Britain and continental Europe. Out of this, the first Keswick Convention was held in 1875.

Keswick theology emphasized a "second blessing" experience but was oriented primarily toward mild Calvinists. It rejected Wesleyan notions of entire sanctification as a "cleansing from sin," offering instead the idea that the second blessing empowered believers in a manner that suppressed sinful behavior. Evangelists in D. L. Moody's circle brought Keswick theology to America where Rev. A. B. Simpson, a Presbyterian, emerged as a primary advocate.

Pentecostal Holiness

As the nineteenth century closed, a fourth holiness channel developed in American religion. In Topeka, Kansas, students in Rev. Charles Parham's Bible school embraced "speaking in tongues" as an "initial evidence" of Holy Spirit baptism. Parham developed a "three works of grace" theology that emphasized experiences of justification, entire sanctification, and a separate Baptism of the Holy Spirit "with tongues following." William Seymour, an African-American, spread this theology through his leadership of Los Angeles' Azusa Street Revival. G. B. Cashwell and others carried this message throughout the South.

Some Pentecostals rejected entire sanctification and dropped it from their order of salvation. They emphasized only a conversion experience and the Baptism of the Holy Spirit. In some respects, their second work of grace was the Keswick view of holiness, with "tongues" added as an evidence of that work.

A Sectarian Heyday

The Wesleyan-Holiness movement splintered in its third generation, divided by rival ecclesiologies, rival eschatologies, lay supervision of holiness venues, divine healing, and women's preaching and leadership.

In time the Wesleyan-Holiness landscape had a cluster of churches that retained their Methodist character, including the Church of the Nazarene, the Free Methodist Church, the Pilgrim Holiness Church, the Church of Christ (Holiness), and the Wesleyan Methodist Church. Around them were churches of non-Methodist origin that had accepted Wesleyan views of grace and holiness, including the Church of God (Anderson, Indiana), Evangelical Friends, Brethren in Christ, and the Missionary Church. Still other churches clustered around the "radical holiness" rubric, such as the Bible Missionary Church, Bible Methodist Church, Church of God (Holiness), and others.

Despite the splintering of the Wesleyan-Holiness forces, a large number – perhaps a majority of Wesleyan-Holiness people – remained loyal to the Methodist Episcopal denominations. There they maintained a consistent witness through a network of holiness camp meetings and through schools, including Asbury College, Taylor University, and Asbury Theological Seminary.

The Keswick movement generated one denomination, the Christian and Missionary Alliance. The Alliance and Wesleyan-Holiness churches have long recognized and affirmed a strong mutual affinity. In Canada, for instance, the Alliance and the Nazarenes jointly operate a liberal arts college.

Pentecostal holiness theology led to several denominations that stress a "three works of grace" theology: the International Pentecostal Holiness Church, the Church of God (Cleveland, Tennessee), and the Church of God in Christ. Two-works Pentecostals have most notably produced the Assemblies of God, the United Pentecostal Church, and the International Church of the Four-Square Gospel.

A Search for Unity in Holiness

The quest for "Unity in Holiness" is a goal toward which holiness people have strived. Organic mergers is one method they have used. The Church of the Nazarene is itself the product of a series of mergers that by 1915 had united seven smaller denominations. The Wesleyan Church was produced by the 1968 merger of the Pilgrim Holiness and Wesleyan Methodist denominations. Across the twentieth century, Free Methodists, Nazarenes, and Wesleyans have gathered up many smaller Wesleyan bodies.

The search for unity has also led to deliberate work across denominational lines. The National (later Christian) Holiness Association brought leaders and laity in Wesleyan-Holiness churches together in worship and fellowship from 1867 until nearly 2000. Since the CHA suspended operations, church officials meet regularly through the Global Wesleyan Alliance, established in 2011 by leaders of eleven denominations. These meetings, however, are closed to the public.

The quest for "unity in holiness" is a goal toward which holiness people have strived. The Wesleyan Holiness Connection is such a unifying entity.

The Wesleyan Holiness Connection is another unifying entity. It strives to identify and promote goals common to the various holiness denominations and welcomes representation from Pentecostal denominations. This volume details the history, life, and significant outreach of the WHC, including its formation of Aldersgate Press.

Since 1994, Wesleyan Holiness Women Clergy has brought together women from many different denominations, including the Salvation Army. Conferences are held every second year. Scholars have also worked together across denominational lines through the Wesleyan Theological Society and the Society for Pentecostal Studies, and the two scholarly societies have held joint meetings every fifth year since 1998.

Select Bibliography

Dayton, Donald W. with Douglas M. Strong. *Rediscovering an Evangelical Heritage.* Grand Rapids: Baker Academics, 2014.

Dieter, Melvin E. *The Holiness Revival of the Nineteenth Century.* Second edition. Lanham, MD and London: Scarecrow Press, 1996.

Stephens, Randall J. *The Fire Spreads: Holiness and Pentecostalism in the American South.* Cambridge, MA and London: Harvard University Press, 2008.

Strong, Douglas M. *Perfectionist Politics.* Syracuse, NY: Syracuse University Press, 1999.

Synan, Vinson. *The Holiness-Pentecostal Tradition: Charismatic Movements in the Twentieth Century.* Grand Rapids: Eerdmans, 1997.

CURRENTS WITHIN THE WESLEYAN HOLINESS STREAM

The Holiness stream of Christianity calls believers to "go on to perfection" in their spiritual lives. The goals include full obedience, maturity of faith, and becoming and doing all that God expects and enables.

Christians committed to living truly holy lives have joined together to support and implement their high calling. Strong personalities, contrasting cultural settings, and historical incidentals have resulted in a range of "holiness denominations" with differing governance structures, ethical expectations, and ministry orientations. Even so, all believe that life in the one Spirit should bring transformation, power, and unity. This belief has brought them to a common table to understand each other better and maximize their impact on a desperately needy world.

The Wesleyan Holiness Connection is a major expression of this common table of dialogue and mutual understanding. The chapters of Section II allow thirteen of the holiness denominations to speak candidly about themselves, where they have come from, where they have gone right and wrong, and what they have to offer to the others.

The Holiness diamond has many facets. Seeing each more clearly helps all to increasingly understand and appreciate the whole.

CHAPTER 6

ASSEMBLIES OF GOD

by Darrin J. Rodgers

T he Assemblies of God was organized in April, 1914, in Hot Springs, Arkansas, in order to provide accountability, structure, and unity so that Pentecostals could better carry out the mission of God in their communities and around the world. This vision transcended racial and social divides and grew to become a multi-ethnic and international movement. The approximately 300 men and women who came together in Hot Springs organized a fellowship that has become one of the largest families of Christian churches in the world.

Early Pentecostal Revival

The Assemblies of God is one of several denominations birthed in the early twentieth-century Pentecostal revival. Embraced was a worldview that emphasized a transformative encounter with God. Pentecostals drew from a tapestry of beliefs within evangelicalism, including a high view of Scripture. Like other Holiness believers, they aimed for full consecration which included separation from sin and a desire to be fully committed to Christ and his mission.

Many adopted the Wesleyan doctrine of entire sanctification, the idea that the believer's desires could be reshaped by the Holy Spirit to become perfect in love. Others embraced the Reformed emphasis on Spirit baptism for empowerment for Christian service. Most

Pentecostals affirmed classic premillennial eschatology which predicted a period of rapid social decay followed by Christ's return. And Pentecostals became some of the more prominent participants in the faith healing movement. While Pentecostals drew from many theological streams within evangelicalism, they formed an identifiable movement because of their common commitment to the experience of baptism in the Holy Spirit. This emphasis on a post-conversion experience was widespread within certain segments of evangelicalism in the nineteenth and early twentieth centuries.

Why did the doctrine and experience of the baptism in the Holy Spirit become attractive to large numbers of people? Because it addressed a basic spiritual longing, the desire to be close to God. Many believers were captivated by the desire for a deeper life in Christ. They were spiritually hungry and desired to be more committed Christ-followers. These ardent seekers saw in Scripture that Spirit baptism provided empowerment for living above normal human existence and witnessing effectively.

> The aim is full consecration, a separation from sin, and a desire to be fully committed to the mission of Christ.

While many sought Spirit baptism, uncertainty existed regarding how to determine whether one had received it. Answering this question, Kansas Holiness evangelist Charles F. Parham identified a scriptural pattern – that the "Bible evidence" (later called the "initial evidence") of Spirit baptism was speaking in tongues. Students at his school in Topeka, Kansas, began speaking in tongues at a prayer meeting in January, 1901. Through his Apostolic Faith movement, Parham had success in promoting the gift of tongues. There had been similar revivals in the late 1800s and early 1900s across the world and throughout church history.[1] But now the 1906 revival at the Apostolic

---

1   Stanley Howard Frodsham, *With Signs Following*, rev. ed. (Springfield, MO: Gospel Publishing House, 1946).

Faith Mission on Azusa Street in Los Angeles catapulted the young movement before a new and larger audience.

William Seymour, an African-American and former student of Parham, led the Azusa Street Mission. The revival lasted for three years, reportedly with non-stop services. This revival brought together men and women from diverse religious, ethnic, and national backgrounds. Participant Frank Bartleman famously exulted that at Azusa Street "the 'color line' was washed away in the blood."[2] Scores of periodicals from around the world carried reports of this revival. As news of the outpouring spread, ministers and lay persons made pilgrimages to Azusa Street to experience the remarkable revival and seek to be baptized in the Holy Spirit.

Participants became known as Pentecostals, named after the Jewish feast of Pentecost when the Holy Spirit was first given to the church and believers first spoke in tongues (Acts 2). It is important to note that Pentecostals viewed tongues as the evidence and not the purpose of Spirit baptism. The purpose is to glorify Christ. William Seymour admonished people at the Azusa Street Mission, "Now, don't go from this meeting and talk about tongues, but try to get people saved."[3]

Formation of the Assemblies of God

Many established churches did not welcome this revival, and participants felt the need to form new congregations. As the revival rapidly spread, many Pentecostals recognized the need for greater organization and accountability. The founding fathers and mothers of the Assemblies of God met in Hot Springs, Arkansas on April, 1914, to promote unity and doctrinal stability, establish legal standing, coordinate the mission enterprise, and establish a ministerial training school. The business

---

2   Frank Bartleman, *How Pentecost Came to Los Angeles* (Los Angeles, CA: the author, 1925), 54.

3   B. F. Lawrence, *The Apostolic Faith Restored* (St. Louis, MO: Gospel Publishing House, 1916), 86.

meeting was called "General Council" and the new body was called the General Council of the Assemblies of God.

The participants at the Hot Springs meeting incorporated the General Council with a hybrid congregational and presbyterian polity. The first two officers elected were Eudorus N. Bell as chairman (title later changed to general superintendent) and J. Roswell Flower as secretary. While most other U.S. Pentecostal denominations were regionally defined, the Assemblies of God claimed a broad nationwide constituency.

Doctrinal Emphases

The Assemblies of God identified with the broader Holiness movement which melded evangelical doctrine with an emphasis on the need for a deeper spiritual life. Salvation and sanctification were primary concerns. No formal theological statement was established at the first General Council, intentionally allowing for some diversity within the bounds of the Holiness worldview. The preamble to the first constitution of the Assemblies of God aimed for unity despite differences: "endeavoring to keep the unity of the Spirit in the bonds of peace, until we all come into the unity of the faith."[4]

> Holiness can be affirmed by eradicationists and those who hold to a progressive view of sanctification.

One of the first major divisions within Pentecostalism involved the issue of sanctification. Some held to a radical Wesleyan view that it is possible for the sin nature to be eradicated following an instantaneous experience of sanctification. Many who disagreed advocated more traditional Wesleyan views (including William Durham's "Finished Work" perspective), contending that

4   General Council Minutes, April, 1914, 4.

sanctification is progressive, not instantaneous, and that perfection is not possible on earth. Most Assemblies of God founders adhered to this latter view.[5]

Assemblies of God leaders quickly realized the need to develop theological boundaries. For instance, they were faced with a new teaching that denied the doctrine of the Trinity. In 1916 the General Council approved a *Statement of Fundamental Truths* that affirmed the fellowship's Trinitarian and evangelical witness. This resulted in the departure of some, including those opposed to what was perceived as "creedalism." Three of the Statement's sixteen sections pertain to sanctification and baptism in the Holy Spirit. Section seven, "Baptism in the Holy Spirit" (as of 2016), reads:

> All believers are entitled to and should ardently expect and earnestly seek the promise of the Father, the baptism in the Holy Spirit and fire, according to the command of our Lord Jesus Christ. This was the normal experience of all in the early Christian church. With it comes the enduement of power for life and service, the bestowment of the gifts and their uses in the work of the ministry (Luke 24:49; Acts 1:4,8; 1 Corinthians 12:1-31). This experience is distinct from and subsequent to the experience of the new birth (Acts 8:12-17; 10:44-46; 11:14-16; 15:7-9). With the baptism in the Holy Spirit come such experiences as an overflowing fullness of the Spirit (John 7:37-39; Acts 4:8), a deepened reverence for God (Acts 2:43; Hebrews 12:28), an intensified consecration to God and dedication to His work (Acts 2:42), and a more active love for Christ, for His Word, and for the lost (Mark 16:20).

---

5   Bruce E. Rosdahl, "The Doctrine of Sanctification in the Assemblies of God" (Ph.D. dissertation, Dallas Theological Seminary, 2008). Rosdahl contends that the "Finished Work" view of sanctification is both Wesleyan and non-eradicationist and is sometimes mischaracterized as Reformed or Baptistic.

Section eight, "The Initial Physical Evidence of the Baptism in the Holy Spirit," reads (as of 2016):

> The baptism of believers in the Holy Spirit is witnessed by the initial physical sign of speaking with other tongues as the Spirit of God gives them utterance (Acts 2:4). The speaking in tongues in this instance is the same in essence as the gift of tongues (1 Corinthians 12:4-10, 28), but different in purpose and use.

Section nine was originally titled "Entire Sanctification." While this term was also used by many Wesleyan Pentecostals who taught that the sinful nature could be instantaneously eradicated, the Assemblies of God's position was ambiguous enough that it could be affirmed by both eradicationists and those who held to a progressive view of sanctification. The section title was renamed "Sanctification" in 1961. As of 2016, Section nine reads:

> Sanctification is an act of separation from that which is evil, and of dedication unto God (Romans 12:1,2; 1 Thessalonians 5:23; Hebrews 13:12). Scriptures teach a life of "holiness without which no man shall see the Lord" (Hebrews 12:14). By the power of the Holy Spirit we are able to obey the command: "Be ye holy, for I am holy" (1 Peter 1:15,16). Sanctification is realized in the believer by recognizing his identification with Christ in His death and resurrection, and by faith reckoning daily upon the fact of that union, and by offering every faculty continually to the dominion of the Holy Spirit (Romans 6:1-11,13; 8:1,2,13; Galatians 2:20; Philippians 2:12,13; 1 Peter 1:5).

Contributions

The Assemblies of God is probably best known for its significant contributions in global missions. Delegates at the second General Council, held in Chicago in November, 1914, resolved to achieve "the greatest evangelism that the world has ever seen."[6] By 1915 the Assemblies of God endorsed approximately thirty missionaries, many of whom had prior affiliations with the Christian and Missionary Alliance or other Holiness organizations.

The Assemblies of God committed itself in 1921 to a missions strategy of establishing self-governing, self-supporting, and self-sustaining churches in missions lands. It adopted this indigenous church principle long before it was embraced by most mainline Protestant groups. In 2014 the World Assemblies of God Fellowship reported over 67 million adherents, now one the largest Protestant families of churches in the world. In 2014, the Assemblies of God reported over 3.1 million U.S. adherents, marking 25 years of continuous growth. Immigrants and ethnic minorities, which now account for over 42% of U.S. adherents, are fueling much of this increase.

Like many other Holiness churches, the Assemblies of God has a long tradition of affirming women in ministry, engaging in ministry across ethnic and social divides, and supporting works of compassion. Its embrace of these themes, often ahead of the broader society, arose from its Holiness worldview. In its origins and when at its best, The Assemblies of God has placed priority on the spiritual life which is lived out in purity of heart and power for witness.

---

6 *General Council Minutes*, November, 1914, 12.

Select Bibliography

Farkas, Thomas George. "William H. Durham and the Sanctification Controversy in Early American Pentecostalism, 1906-1916." Ph.D. thesis, Southern Baptist Theological Seminary, 1993.

McGee, Gary B. *People of the Spirit: The Assemblies of God* [rev. ed.]. Springfield, MO: Gospel Publishing House, 2014.

Menzies, Robert E. *Empowered for Witness: The Spirit in Luke-Acts*. New York: T&T Clark, 2004.

Menzies, William W. and Stanley M. Horton. *Bible Doctrines: A Pentecostal Perspective*. Springfield, MO: Gospel Publishing House, 1993.

Rosdahl, Bruce E. "The Doctrine of Sanctification in the Assemblies of God." Ph.D. dissertation, Dallas Theological Seminary, 2008.

Williams, E. S. *Systematic Theology*. Springfield, MO: Gospel Publishing House, 1953.

CHAPTER 7

THE BRETHREN IN CHRIST

by E. Morris Sider

Around 1780, two historic movements, Anabaptism and Pietism, came together in Lancaster County, Pennsylvania, resulting in the origin of the Brethren in Christ. These two visions of the Christian life have characterized the Brethren throughout its long history.

Anabaptism and Pietism Join

Mennonites, one of the groups descending from sixteenth-century Anabaptists, largely comprised the founders of the new group that became know as the Brethren in Christ. The founders brought with them such Anabaptist insights as the believer's church (involving adult baptism),[1] separation from the world in such areas as politics and dress, obedience to biblical truth, and the centrality of Christian community. They based these principles on the life and teachings of Jesus as found in the four Gospels.

The founders encountered Pietism in the late 1700s in meetings conducted by Pietist evangelists Philip Otterbein and Martin Boehme (a former Mennonite minister). In these meetings they received crisis conversions, experiences then unknown to Mennonites who considered

---

1   See Barry L. Callen, *Radical Christianity: The Believers' Church Tradition in Christianity's History and Future* (Evangel Press, 1999).

that entry into the Christian life came through nurture by the family and the congregation. Their new experiences led the group to meet together to discuss their new life in Christ and to explore what other truths they might discover in Scripture. Their search led to the conviction that baptism should be by immersion (as Mennonites they had been baptized by pouring). When they could find no minister to baptize them in this manner, they baptized themselves. This baptism was the catalyst in their decision to remain together as a new body of believers. At first called River Brethren, they renamed themselves Brethren in Christ in the mid-nineteenth century.

> Anabaptism and Pietism are visions of the Christian life that have characterized the Brethren throughout its history.

To their Anabaptist views the founders wedded the thought and practices of Pietism. Concern for a right relationship with God was expressed in private devotions, extemporaneous prayers, and testimony meetings in which members related accounts of their walk with God. This was the experiential nature of their Christian lives. From their beginning the Brethren in Christ synthesized the experiential nature of Pietism with the ethical nature of Anabaptism.

The Coming of Holiness Teaching

Beginning around 1880 and for over a period of some thirty years, dramatic developments took place among the Brethren in Christ. The changes affirmed and even strengthened the Anabaptist-Pietist synthesis. Basic to these developments was the Brethren's acceptance of holiness as expressed in the American holiness movement. From their beginning, the Brethren had emphasized the Pietist experiential nature of the Christian life; holiness clearly was of that nature. Moreover, they had been singing from their unannotated hymnals songs of a more holy life as taught by the Wesleys. Also, their Anabaptism taught them that a more holy life was achieved by walking in obedience and journeying toward holiness. However, the teaching that the Brethren were now hearing offered a quicker way to holiness than did the journey of Anabaptism.

Contact with the holiness movement came through some association with the Salvation Army and the Church of the Nazarene, but most significantly with the Hepzibah Faith Missionary Society and its school in Iowa. Some Brethren in Christ young people attended the school in preparation for missionary work abroad. They accepted the strong holiness emphasis of the school and took their enthusiasm back to their home congregations. Church leaders, such as Noah Zook and John R. Zook, also developed a strong connection with the Hepzibah group. Convinced of the biblical soundness of holiness as promoted by these groups, they spread the message across the Brethren in Christ world in Canada and the United States through highly popular revival meetings. Giving support to these efforts were the pages of the *Evangelical Visitor*, the church paper widely read by the church's members. By 1910 the doctrine was officially sanctioned by action of General Conference, the governing body of the denomination.

Growing acceptance of the doctrine helped to inspire other very significant changes. The Brethren in Christ initiated foreign missionary work in Africa and India, began Sunday schools, established a school (now Messiah College), inaugurated a church paper, and produced a new, more spirited hymnal with musical notations. Clearly the Holy Spirit was at work among the Brethren in Christ.

The Expanding Influence of Holiness

The years following 1910 brought an expansion and consolidation of the holiness doctrine. Teaching on holiness found a home in several camp meetings. Roxbury Holiness Camp in Pennsylvania began in 1936. Other camps were established in Ontario (Niagara Holiness Camp) and in Ohio (Memorial Holiness Camp), followed by a camp in Florida (Camp Freedom) in the early 1960s.

Also in these years, the Brethren in Christ formulated their strongest statement on holiness. The 1937 edition of the *Manual of Doctrine and Government* declared that holiness was obtained through sanctification, an act of grace subsequent to conversion, which now keeps the believer clean from the defilement of a sinful world. The statement reads in part:

> When a sinner after a thorough evangelical repentance, receives pardon for his sins, he is "born again" and becomes a new creature (2 Cor. 5:17). As such he is placed in a new kingdom and enjoys a holy life to the extent that he abhors his past sins and earnestly strives to live this holy life. He does not wittingly or deliberately commit sin (1 Jn. 3:9). However, carnality remaining in the newborn babe in Christ produces manifestations (1 Cor. 3:1-3), which will cause him to loathe this condition and long for complete deliverance (Rom. 7:24; Heb. 2:15). This deliverance is received in the experience of sanctification which is obtained instantaneously and subsequent to the new birth (Jas. 4:8; 2 Cor. 7:1; Eph. 5:25-27) . . . . The believer is now kept clean from the defilement of a sinful world, which he must contact continually in his social, commercial, and religious activities, as he walks in the light of God's Word (1 Jn. 1:7) in continual obedience and complete surrender to His will. He is now in a better position to "grow in grace and in the knowledge of our Lord and Saviour Jesus Christ."

Later Years

The Brethren in Christ has initiated further change since the middle of the twentieth century. Restrictions relating to worldly entertainment and plain dress have been relaxed. New worship styles, including the use of musical instruments in worship services, were accepted and a more ecumenical stance was taken, as evidenced by membership and leadership roles in such organizations as the National Association of Evangelicals, the National Holiness Association, and now the Wesleyan Holiness Connection.

> Brethren accepted holiness and always have emphasized the experiential nature of the Christian life.

These changes were accompanied by a shift in the denomination's position on holiness. While the view of holiness as an act of grace subsequent to conversion remains the conviction of many members, other members now take a more Anabaptist approach to holiness. The image of the journey is basic to this view, but the view also recognizes that at times along the way the Christian may have a significant encounter with the Holy Spirit that empowers her or him better to do God's will. Note the 2014 edition of the *Manual of Doctrine and Government*:

> We believe that God's grace provides for more than forgiveness of sin. As the Spirit works in the life of the believer, he or she is led forward in sanctification to a full surrender and commitment of the motives and will to Christ. This results in freedom from the control of sin and in empowerment to live the holy life. The Holy Spirit fills persons yielded to God and equips them for effective witness and service. Sanctification is also an ongoing journey of yielding to God and growing in grace. The quality of the surrendered life corresponds to the believer's responsiveness to the Holy Spirit and obedience to the Word of God.

Ongoing Contributions

The call to holiness has engaged Brethren in Christ in such activities as relief work (through Mennonite Central Committee), sponsorship of retirement homes, and engagement in social services. The denomination's peace position has as a foundation the view that holiness means loving not only fellow Christians but also even our enemies.

Another noteworthy contribution of the denomination is the marked degree to which the Holy Spirit has inspired mission work. Although the denomination has only a little more than 30,000 members in the United States and Canada, it has developed missions and churches in over twenty countries. It should come as no surprise that many Brethren in Christ missionaries over the years have related that their call to Christian service came by the prompting of the Holy Spirit. Naturally, then, the recent rise of the Wesleyan Holiness Connection has been applauded by the Brethren in Christ.

Select Bibliography

Byers, Charlie B., *Steps to Victorious Living* (Elizabethtown, Pa.: McBeth Press, 1952).

Keefer, Luke L., *Everything Necessary: God's Provision for the Holy Life* (Nappanee, IN: Evangel Press, 1984).

Sider, E. Morris, *A Living and Growing Ministry: The Story of the Roxbury Holiness Camp* (Roxbury, PA: Roxbury Holiness Camp, 2010).

Wittlinger, Carlton Oscar, *Quest for Piety and Obedience: The Story of the Brethren in Christ* (Nappanee, IN: Evangel Press, 1978), chapters XI and XIV.

Zook, John Roel, *Holiness and Empowerment: Both Defined, How to Obtain Them and How to Retain Them* (Des Moines, IA: Kenyon Printing and Manufacturing Company, n.d. [around 1906]).

CHAPTER 8

THE CHRISTIAN & MISSIONARY ALLIANCE

by Bernie A. Van De Walle

The Christian and Missionary Alliance is an Evangelical Christian denomination whose historic theological emphasis has been the Fourfold Gospel – Christ, Our Savior, Sanctifier, Healer, and Coming King. Its stated practical foci have been two: the promotion and cultivation of the Deeper Life and the evangelization of the world, with particular attention to the "least-reached."

Origins

The earliest leaders and members of The Christian & Missionary Alliance represented the theological and ecclesial diversity of late nineteenth-century American Evangelicalism. Among them were Presbyterians, Methodists, Anglicans, Salvationists, Baptists, and Anabaptists.

The formation of The Christian and Missionary Alliance (often "the C&MA" or "the Alliance") began primarily in the ministry of Albert Benjamin Simpson (1843–1919), a Canadian-born former Presbyterian minister (Hamilton, ON; Louisville, KY; and New York City, NY) and founding pastor of the independent Gospel Tabernacle (1882) in New York City. After resigning his Presbyterian ministry because of a change of conviction regarding the legitimacy of baptizing infants and his recent adoption of a premillennial eschatology, Simpson set out to evangelize the unreached immigrant masses of New York City.

Simpson, who had gained substantial notoriety from an itinerant speaking and publishing ministry, also operated a series of Christian conventions. These gatherings promoted the various tenets of the Fourfold Gospel, culminating with a grand missions rally. One particular gathering in 1886 agreed that those assembled should reconvene one year later to form an organization that would have as its explicit goals the promotion of the Deeper Life and, especially, the evangelization of the world. The next summer this convention reconvened at Old Orchard Beach, Maine, where two organizations formally came into existence: The Christian Alliance and The Evangelical Missionary Alliance.

Among its stated objectives, The Christian Alliance existed to promote the Deeper Life and to "lead the children of God into the practical experience of all the fullness of Jesus," including "Complete Sanctification through Christ for all who fully yield themselves to Him." Beyond that, early members of the organization agreed "to pray for each other daily for the sanctification of believers . . . ." Its sister organization, The Evangelical Missionary Alliance, existed "to carry the Gospel 'to all nations,' with special reference to the needs of the destitute and unoccupied fields of the heathen world." For various

Emphasized is the Fourfold Gospel— Christ, Our Savior, Sanctifier, Healer, and Coming King.

reasons, both practical and theological, these two organizations came together in 1897 to form The Christian and Missionary Alliance.

These two Alliances were never to be considered denominations or to compete with those denominations already in existence. Rather, they were intended to exist as para-church organizations providing for their members opportunities to pursue and promote the Deeper Life and missions supplemental to those provided by their home churches. Regardless, it was not long before the success of the C&MA led many local congregations and individual ministers to associate themselves with it, practically establishing it as a denomination. In spite of this practical reality, the Alliance formally resisted the denominational label well into the middle of the twentieth century.

The Holiness Emphasis

Given its historic desire to include "Evangelical Christians of every name," The Alliance was, and continues to be, "middle-of-the-road" in doctrine and temperament. Yet, from its inception, it recognized that "there are special truths which . . . need to be doubly emphasized." These compose what Simpson and others called the Fourfold Gospel. They are: 1. Conversion; 2. Sanctification; 3. Divine Healing; and 4. Premillennialism. While sanctification was only one of the four "special truths," it was said to have "a special relevance to the identity of The Christian and Missionary Alliance. No emphasis had a greater influence on its founding. It shaped its development and was a prime element in the selection of its priorities."[1]

A. B. Simpson's teaching on sanctification is both voluminous and extensive. The intentional interdenominational and international character of The Christian and Missionary Alliance, however, has meant that the denomination has a less extensive doctrine of sanctification than does its founder. Consequently, to identify what the founder taught on this particular issue is not necessarily to identify what the denomination has either held or currently holds.

The denomination[2] has historically emphasized both the doctrine of holiness and certain views in relation to it. In typical Holiness Movement fashion, The C&MA asserts that holiness, rather than being

---

1   Samuel J. Stoesz, *Sanctification: An Alliance Distinctive* (Camp Hill, PA: Christian Publications, 1992), 5.

2   It should be noted that each national church in The C&MA is autonomous and, therefore, there is no Statement of Faith or, consequently, statement on the doctrine of sanctification that governs them all. For the most part, however, what is asserted, especially in regard to sanctification, is similar if not essentially the same.

a soteriological appendage, is normative for God's people. Holiness is God's will and desire for all of people and not just a select few. Second, sanctification is a work of the Holy Spirit who initiates it in an event called "the baptism of the Holy Spirit." Third, the Alliance asserts that sanctification also begins in a "crisis," a definitive act of faith on the part of the believer. Furthermore, echoing typical Wesleyan teaching, this crisis is understood to occur subsequent to conversion. Finally, the Alliance holds that, flowing from this crisis, holiness is realized both progressively and over a period of time.

> The deeper life of holiness validates and empowers mission.

While The C&MA's holiness emphasis is sure, its theological position is notoriously difficult to classify, at least according to traditional categories. Even within the denomination, the question of its proper categorization continues to be a topic of disagreement. In spite of the fact that Simpson's own experience of sanctification was typical of the Holiness pattern, and though Simpson spoke at significant Holiness events, including the Bethshan Conference for Holiness and Healing (1885) where he delivered his signature sermon, "Himself," Simpson noted, "We believe that the Alliance teaching on [sanctification] is neither Wesleyan nor, strictly speaking, an echo of even the excellent teaching given at the meetings annually held at Keswick."

Adding to this difficulty is the fact that some language employed by the Alliance, while it invokes Wesleyan themes, refers to something distinct. For example, while Simpson and The C&MA employ the phrases "wholly sanctified" and "complete sanctification," one should not assume this means what Wesleyans intend by the phrases "Christian perfection" or "entire sanctification." While the latter terms refer to the intensive possibility of sanctification – that is, the degree to which one can expect to be made holy in this life, the terms employed by the Alliance are intended to denote the extensive nature of sanctification, that the sanctifying work of God applies to the entirety of the fallen human condition.

This statement should be noted from the "Statement of Faith of The Christian & Missionary Alliance" (United States):

> It is the will of God that each believer should be filled with the Holy Spirit and be sanctified wholly (1 Thess. 5:23), being separated from sin and the world and fully dedicated to the will of God, thereby receiving power for holy living and effective service (Acts 1:8). This is both a crisis and a progressive experience wrought in the life of the believer subsequent to conversion (Rom. 6:1–14).

Distinctive Contributions

Historically, The C&MA's particular contribution to the Holiness Movement may be found in its Christocentric emphasis. While the Holy Spirit is explicitly described as the agent of the believer's growth in holiness, the Alliance has placed a particular emphasis on the central and indispensable role that Christ plays in that same work. For the Alliance, as for many other Christian traditions, Christ is the *measure* of holiness. That is, in the incarnation, Christ has demonstrated for us true holiness.

Yet, for the Alliance, Christ is also the *means* of the believer's holiness. That is, for The C&MA, the holiness of the believer is not the result of either the imputation or importation of a commodity known as holiness. Instead, the holiness of the believer is nothing other than the overflowing of the holiness of the very person of the indwelling Christ Himself.

Beyond that, the Alliance has consistently emphasized that there is a necessary and natural link between its two historic practical foci: the Deeper Life and world-wide evangelism. First, holiness both validates and empowers those on mission. Second, those who are being conformed to the image of Christ are being conformed to his desires and agendas, and, therefore, are compelled "to seek and to save those who are lost." Finally, while obedience to the Great Commission has served as a motivation for the Alliance's missionary activity, historically its foremost motivation was the hope that, upon the completion of the evangelization of the world, Christ, the Holy One, will return and "we shall be like him."

Select Bibliography

McGraw, Gerald E., "The Doctrine of Sanctification in the Published Writings of Albert Benjamin Simpson." Ph.D. diss., New York University, 1986.

Niklaus, Robert L., John S. Sawin, and Samuel J. Stoesz, *All for Jesus: God at Work in The Christian and Missionary Alliance for More Than 125 Years.* 2nd ed. Colorado Springs: Christian and Missionary Alliance, 2013.

Pardington, George P., *The Crisis of the Deeper Life.* New York: Christian Alliance Publishing Co., 1906.

Simpson, Albert B., *The Fourfold Gospel.* New York: Word, Work, and World Publishing Co., 1888.

Simpson, Albert B., *The Highest Christian Life: Expositions of the Epistle to the Ephesians.* South Nyack, NY: Christian Alliance Publishing Co., 1898.

Simpson, Albert B., *A Larger Christian Life.* New York: Christian Alliance Publishing Co., 1890.

Simpson, Albert B., *The Self-Life and the Christ-Life.* South Nyack, NY: Christian Alliance Publishing Co., 1897.

Simpson, Albert B., *Wholly Sanctified.* New York: Christian Alliance Publishing Co., 1893.

Stoesz, Samuel J., *Sanctification: An Alliance Distinctive*. Camp Hill, PA: Christian Publications, 1992.

Tozer, Aiden W., *Man: The Dwelling Place of God, The Pursuit of God*, and *The Knowledge of the Holy*. Harrisburg, PA: Christian Publications, 1966.

Tozer, Aiden W., *The Pursuit of God*. Harrisburg, PA: Christian Publications, 1948.

Van De Walle, Bernie A., *The Heart of the Gospel: A. B. Simpson, the Fourfold Gospel, and Late Nineteenth-Century Evangelical Theology*. Eugene, OR: Wipf and Stock, 2009.

CHAPTER 9

THE CHURCH OF GOD
(ANDERSON, IN)

by Barry L. Callen

The Church of God movement (Anderson) is a Christian reform movement dedicated to a return to central biblical teachings and serious Christian living. Its historic roots lie deep in the Wesleyan and "Radical" traditions of Christianity. Many of its earliest adherents in the last two decades of the nineteenth century were former Methodists and Mennonites. They were vigorous church reformers driven by their passion for the restored holiness and unity of the people of God.

Context and Beginnings

Following the Civil War of the 1860s, the religious scene in the United States was dominated by a neglect and even denial of much that previously had been held as basic within the Christian community. The Church of God movement, part of the larger Holiness Movement, emerged in the 1880s. It was committed particularly to restoring the integrity of the church through a return to the acceptance of biblical authority and unity among believers through the common experience of holiness. As a "reformation" movement, it sought to "come out" of the compromising and competitive chaos of divisive and self-seeking denominationalism.

The thought world of the Church of God has a direct link to John Winebrenner's reforming efforts in the early nineteenth century. More broadly, it derives from two major Christian traditions, the Wesleyan and the "Radical" (Anabaptist) – the particular themes of which are summarized below. The first major publication of the new movement was the 1880 release of the book *Bible Proofs of the Second Work of Grace* by the movement's primary pioneer, Daniel S. Warner.

> The pioneers were driven by their passion for the restored holiness and unity of God's people.

Since the Holiness Movement of that time was focused on holiness restoration and not on a resolving of the denominational dividedness of the church, the Church of God movement often was a strident come-out voice on the fringes of the larger restoration efforts. Warner wrote this in his personal journal in March, 1878: ". . . the Lord showed me that holiness could never prosper upon sectarian soil encumbered by human creeds and party names, and he gave me a new commission to join holiness and all truth together and build up the apostolic church of the living God."

Movement pioneers like Warner spoke of the "early morning light" shining again in the "evening time" of the church's troubled history.[1] They sought to restore a free and open fellowship of sanctified believers bound together by love and shared holiness instead of by divisive creeds and self-serving church organizations called denominations.

Central Teachings

The central teachings of the Church of God movement typically were sung enthusiastically rather than framed in formalized creedal statements that always are limited and tend to be divisive. Instead, this holiness-unity vision was sung in congregations and camp meetings across the land:

---

1   See Robert H. Reardon, *The Early Morning Light* (Warner Press, 1979; reprint, Reformation Publishers, 2014).

We reach our hands in fellowship
To every blood-washed one,
While love entwines about each heart
In which God's will is done.[2]

And again:

How sweet this bond of perfectness,
The wondrous love of Jesus!
A pure foretaste of heaven's bliss,
O fellowship so precious!
Beloved, how this perfect love
Unites us all in Jesus!
One heart, and soul, and mind we prove
The union heaven gave us.[3]

Note the emphasis love that reaches out. Focus was on experienced holiness ("perfect love") as the key to Christian unity.

The fellowship of the church is understood to be all of the redeemed. The unity of the church is essential for effective mission and is enabled only as the love of God (the shared holiness of the divine) binds believers together and sends them out. Thus, the classic published history of the Church of God movement is titled *The Quest for Holiness and Unity*.[4] Its teaching emphases are detailed in the book *Contours of a Cause*.[5] They include core elements of the Wesleyan and Radical (Anabaptist) teaching traditions, namely:

---

2   Verse three of the hymn "The Church's Jubilee" composed in 1923 by Charles Naylor and Andrew Byers, intending to reflect the prayer of Jesus for unity (Jn. 17:23).

3   Verse one and chorus of the hymn "The Bond of Perfectness," lyrics by Daniel Warner.

4   John W. V. Smith, *The Quest for Holiness and Unity* (Warner Press, 1980, rev. ed. 2009).

5   Barry L. Callen, *Contours of a Cause* (Anderson School of Theology, 1995).

1. Voluntary adult membership based on a covenant-commitment to Jesus Christ.

2. A community of discipline, edification, and correction in conscious separation from the world.

3. A life of good works, service, and witness as an expression of Christian love.

4. The Spirit and the Word as comprising the sole basis of authority, with a corresponding de-emphasis on the roles of church traditions and creeds.

5. Focus on restoring the essential elements of early church life and practice that thrived prior to the many compromises seen in later church history.

6. A pragmatic, functional approach to church order and structure.

7. Belief in the universal church as the body of Christ, with individual communities of believers being visible parts.

Classic Statements of Belief

Since the Church of God movement has no official creed (its typical affirmation is "no creed but the Bible"), note the following statements on holiness from four of its highly respected leaders.

1. Having perceived that this "second grace" is the ultimate end of Christ's death, and the great burden of the apostolic ministry, I was constrained to dedicate forever

unto the Lord all the energies of my being for the promotion of this great salvation.[6]

2. The doctrine of sanctification has been abused so badly
by its advocates and ridiculed so thoroughly by its op-
ponents that few modern scholars care to plunge into
the welter of fanaticism and passionate strife with which
the subject is involved. To the present writer this seems
a great pity and certain tragic loss . . . . The doctrine of
sanctification is for Christian people the most important of all the doctrines because it teaches the way to
find and to develop faith in Christ as the perfect healer
of the heart, who alone can make it entirely well and fill
it with the enduring strength of his Holy Spirit.[7]

3. Entire sanctification refers to the completed process
by which the Holy Spirit makes his home in the human soul. It does not mean that the process of spiritual
growth has been completed . . . . Rather, it means that
the person is wholly committed to God, and that the
Holy Spirit has accepted the invitation to dwell in the
soul and do all he comes to do . . . . The completeness
of sanctification has to do with the completeness of our
relationship to God, a relationship of perfect love.[8]

4. In his 1950 *Requiem for a Nun*, William Faulkner
writes one of his more famous lines: "The past is never
dead. It's not even past." So it is with holiness. This

6   Daniel S. Warner, *Bible Proofs of the Second Work of Grace* (1880), 9.

7   Charles E. Brown, *The Meaning of Sanctification* (Warner Press, 1945, rev. ed. 2014).

8   Kenneth E. Jones, *The Commitment to Holiness* (Warner Press, 1985), 118-119.

vital subject has a long history in the faith of Christians and Jews before them, a history hoping to rush to the surface of the present, very much alive and still wanting to be received, breathed, and exercised to make possible a distinctive life for believers. Christian holiness necessarily involves the transformation of believers into truly new persons in Christ. The past of Jesus Christ is never dead and must not be allowed to be only the past. The future depends on it being *our present.*[9]

Core Contributions

Central to the contribution of the Church of God movement to the larger church is its linking of experienced and lived holiness to the unity of the church which is key to effective church mission. God expects and enables the holiness of individuals *and of the church* (to be seen in its biblical faithfulness and unity). A continuation of this distinctive contribution is now threatened by the movement's own tendency to be absorbed in the larger "evangelical" world, a danger facing any open fellowship, and by the general lack of interest in the particulars of church history and theology.

The movement was ahead of the Christian curve with its nineteenth-century concern for the two great issues that consumed the church worldwide in the twentieth century, life in the Spirit (pentecostalism) and ecumenism (overcoming the dividedness of God's people for the sake of church mission). The Church of God remained on the fringes of these broader movements, mistrusting the experiential extremes of some "Pentecostals" and the organizational preoccupation and doctrinal reductionism of some of the ecumenical efforts (World Council of Churches, National Council of Churches, etc.). That

---

9   Barry L. Callen, *Catch Your Breath!* (Aldersgate Press, 2014), 19.

hesitancy to be involved has begun to lessen with the movement's active role in the Wesleyan Holiness Connection.

The movement also has been ahead of most Christian bodies in its active reaching out to all of God's children regardless of gender, skin color, or denominational label. Women have been respected movement leaders from the beginning. African-American believers have been present in substantial numbers, responding to the call for an open fellowship that reaches to "every blood-washed one . . . in which God's will is done."[10] It also has determined to find the best model of a pragmatic, functional approach to church order and structure. No success is claimed, but the intentional search has been public and productive.

> God expects and enables the holiness of individuals *and the church.* The goal is becoming "saints" who experience and express holiness.

Movement leader Charles E. Brown has provided the whole of God's people with important perspective. He wrote this in 1940, and well might have just yesterday! "We seem to live in an age where the caravans of Christianity are glad to rest, each in its little oasis of methods, budgets, building programs, and regular services – counting its gains in percentages, glad enough to break even, anxious to keep the goodwill of the public . . . forgetting entirely the high calls of selfless service and deathless devotion which have hummed in the ears of all the great saints of the past."[11]

In a broken world, the church no longer can be satisfied with being a compromised and divided body. The goal is becoming "saints" who experience and express holiness, and who do it in "perfect love" with each other as they seek together to share this love of Christ with all who are lost.

---

10   James Earl Massey, *African Americans and the Church of God* (Anderson, Indiana) (2005).

11   Charles E. Brown, "Objective of the Reformation," *Gospel Trumpet*, May 4, 1940.

CHAPTER 10

CHURCH OF GOD
(CLEVELAND, TN)

by David G. Roebuck

T he Church of God (Cleveland) is a Wesleyan Pentecostal denomination with ministries in 183 nations and territories of the world
as of 2016. The denomination began as a Baptist reformation movement but transformed into a holiness church toward the end of the
nineteenth century, and then into a Pentecostal one in the early twentieth century. Its foundational commitment is to "the whole Bible rightly
divided," with the New Testament as its "only rule for government and
discipline."[1]

History and Theological Development
The Church of God began in 1886 when R. G. Spurling and his fa-
ther Richard established a "Christian Union" congregation in Monroe
County, Tennessee.[2] The young Spurling believed that the Landmark

---

1   *Church of God Book of Discipline, Church Order and Governance* (Church of God Publishing House,
     2014), 20.

2   For the best history of the birth and early theological development of the Church of God, see Wade
     H. Phillips, *Quest to Restore God's House, A Theological History of the Church of God (Cleveland,
     Tennessee), Volume 1, 1886-1923,* and *R. G. Spurling to A J. Tomlinson, Formation-Transformation-
     Reformation* (CPT Press, 1914). See also Charles W. Conn, *Like a Mighty Army: A History of the Church of*

Baptist theology which dominated that region had excluded Christians from the church based on human creeds. He desired to establish a church based solely on the New Testament. Within a decade of its founding, a holiness revival across the state line in nearby Cherokee County, North Carolina, brought holiness doctrine to the region. Following a long season of revival and persecution in which many were excluded from their Baptist churches for their emphasis on holiness, Spurling organized a congregation in the Camp Creek, North Carolina, home of W. F. Bryant that went by the name Holiness Church.

The Fire-Baptized Holiness Movement was influential in western North Carolina and eastern Tennessee. Several of those congregations came under the influence of leading pastor A. J. Tomlinson. In 1907 the denomination adopted the name "Church of God" as part of its commitment to restore a Biblical church. While there had been Pentecostal manifestations following the holiness revival in 1896, the denomination fully embraced a Pentecostal theology by 1908.

The holiness foundation of the Church of God manifested itself in a commitment to love God and neighbor, cultivate a godly lifestyle, and care for others. In his book *The Lost Link*, founder R. G. Spurling emphasized that God's church had been established on the great commandments to love God and love others. Yet, through Christian history, many had replaced these simple commands with human creeds and traditions. Thus, the Church of God was founded to restore a church based on love, with the only laws being those found in the New Testament.[3]

The holiness emphasis on love manifested itself in right relationships. One of the meaningful testimonies from the 1896 Shearer Schoolhouse revival is that of W. F. Bryant. When the doctrine of sanctification was being preached, Bryant saw something in the lives of

---

God, 1886-1996 (Pathway Press, 2008), and Bill George, *Until All Have Heard: The Centennial History of Church of God World Missions*, (Church of God World Missions, 2010).

3   R. G. Spurling, *The Lost Link* (by author, 1920).

those who testified they were sanctified that made him want the same experience. He later remembered, "At this time I was a member of the Baptist church and none of us believed in sanctification, although I attended this revival. I noticed how those who claimed sanctification would go to their fellowmen and fix everything right, making their confession to one another . . . . I began seeking God definitely for an experience I had never attained to. The spirit within me would cry out, 'Give me the blessing like those other few have received.'" He received and his heart was changed.[4]

Such love propelled the Church of God to care for the whole person, including spiritual, mental, and physical health. Early members searched the Scriptures for biblical instruction on godly living. Long before the medical establishment recognized its dangers, the first Church of God General Assembly in 1906 engaged in a discussion of tobacco within the context of a Christian response to a fallen world. Delegates noted that the use of tobacco was offensive, unhealthy, a bad influence for youth, and a poor use of finances. Further, money spent on tobacco could better be used "to clothe the poor, spread the gospel or make the homes of our country more comfortable."

Lacking a specific biblical reference prohibiting tobacco, and while living in a geographical region in which tobacco was popular and widely accepted among churches, delegates agreed they could not believe Christ would use it. Despite their emphatic opposition to the use of tobacco, they called for church leaders to "deal tenderly and lovingly" with those who use it while also holding them accountable for their actions.[5]

Commitment is to "the whole Bible rightly divided," with the New Testament the "only rule for government and discipline."

4   W. F. Bryant, quoted in "History of Pentecost," *The Faithful Standard* (September, 1922), 6.

5   *Minutes of Annual Assembly* (1906, 5-6).

The Church of God expressed its love for others and the realization that Christians cannot separate the physical and spiritual through continuing efforts to meet the economic and social challenges of the Southern Appalachian Mountains. A. J. Tomlinson operated a school, orphanage, and clothing distribution center as early as 1901, and today the Church of God supports orphanages in many countries of the world. Distributing clothing was a central activity in the denomination's formational years, and today ministries such as Operation Compassion continue to supply the needs of those ravaged by uncontrolled circumstances from poverty to natural disasters.

With its considerable growth, the Church of God has developed ministries to make disciples and reach the harvest. These ministries are organized in five divisions. Care, Discipleship, Education, Support Services, and World Evangelization. 1. Care includes support for chaplains, ministers, immigrants to Israel, orphans, and retired persons. 2. Discipleship ministries focus on men, women, and youth as well as publishing the *Church of God Evangel* and other resources through Pathway Press.

Along with Lee University and the Pentecostal Theological Seminary in Cleveland, Tennessee, 3. Education Ministries encompass ministerial training and connection with more than 200 international institutions. 4. Support Services provides oversight of ministerial retirement benefits and denominational record-keeping as well as maintenance of the International Offices. Finally, 5. World Evangelization gives oversight to evangelism and missions efforts in the U.S.A., Canada, and 181 other countries.

Holiness: Differences and Renewed Commitment

Although the early Church of God was emphatic in opposition to creeds, the movement was not without attention to doctrine. As an example, an early listing of prominent teachings designed to assist ministerial candidates included "sanctification subsequent to the new birth" and "holiness." The statement on Spirit baptism related this experience to the necessity of sanctification: "Baptism with the Holy Ghost subsequent to cleansing . . . ." Biblical references accompanied each of these teachings with the understanding that ministerial candidates and other readers would be able to sufficiently understand these doctrines by reading the cited biblical passages.

Over time, however, theological differences emerged within the Church of God over the timing and nature of sanctification in the life of the believer. To resolve these differences, the denomination adopted a "Declaration of Faith" in 1948 as its primary theological statement. This declaration includes three important statements related to its holiness commitments:

- We believe in sanctification subsequent to the new birth, through faith in the blood of Christ; through the Word, and by the Holy Ghost.

- We believe Holiness to be God's standard of living for His people.

- We believe in the baptism with the Holy Ghost subsequent to a clean heart.

As a movement committed to searching the Scriptures, the Church of God has continually evaluated how to pastorally express a practical commitment to holy living in church and society. Earlier statements listing behaviors the denomination eschewed have been replaced with "Practical Commitments" promoting spiritual example, moral purity, personal integrity, family responsibility, behavioral temperance, modest appearance, and social obligations.

The denomination has also repeatedly affirmed a "Resolution Relative to the Principles of Holiness," including the proclamations: "Be it resolved that we, the Church of God, reaffirm our standard of holiness, in stated doctrine, in principles of conduct, and as a living reality in our hearts; and be it further resolved that we, the Church of God, believe a life of holiness is a balanced life in spirit, mind, and body, and that it places the believer in a Christ-like relationship to God and fellowmen . . . ."[6]

With such affirmations, the Church of God is naturally pleased to recognize and participate in the Wesleyan Holiness Connection, a fresh movement across church life for re-emphasizing the power of holiness to renew the Body of Christ in today's culture.

The Ongoing Challenge

As the Church of God continually reaffirms its commitment to holiness, it calls the Christian church to recognize that holiness is God's standard of living for the people of Jesus Christ. God is holy, and thus those that are in Christ Jesus must also be holy. In this way, Christians demonstrate to the world the very nature of God. Further, sanctification is our provision for living a holy life. In sanctification we are purged from sin and predisposed to love God and to love others. This purging is an answer to Christ's prayer in John 17 that we will be sanctified by his Word (v. 17).

> A life of holiness places the believer in a Christ-like relationship to God and fellowmen.

It is important to add that such sanctification does not take us out of the world but sends us into the world and enables Christians to live in the world free from the evil one (vv. 15 and 18). Indeed, Jesus prayer was not simply for the disciples but for all who follow him throughout the ages (v. 20). Just as the Father and Son are one, Christians are one, and in their oneness reflect the nature and love of God to the world (vv. 21-23).

---

6   *Book of Discipline, Church Order, and Governance*, 17-34.

Finally, the church in community must continually search the Word of God for insight and revelation as to how to apply God's Word to the practical realities of an ever-changing culture. In community we give witness to the love of God expressed to us in redemption and through us in the proclamation of the gospel that God so loved the world that he sent his Son.

CHAPTER 11

THE CHURCH OF THE NAZARENE

by Steven Hoskins

The Church of the Nazarene is a Protestant Christian denomination in the Wesleyan-Holiness tradition committed to making Christlike disciples in the nations. Founded in 1907-08 as an international church, it now numbers over 29,000 congregations and 2.4 million members in over 150 world areas, making it the largest denomination among the Holiness churches and movements.

The doctrines of the Church of the Nazarene are classically orthodox, taking their cues from historic Methodism and its founder, John Wesley, with an emphasis on the doctrine of Christian Perfection or Entire Sanctification. Throughout its history, the ministries of the Nazarene church have emphasized missionary service, compassionate ministry, education, and evangelism.[1]

Historical Overview

The Church of the Nazarene began as a uniting of regionally-based holiness churches, groups, and movements from across the United States. The earliest parent groups included the Association of Pentecostal Churches of America (APCA) with roots in New England and New

---

1   For the current statistics of the Church of the Nazarene, see http://nazarene.org/nazarene-at-a-glance on the Church of the Nazarene's official website, http://nazarene.org.

York, The Holiness Church of Christ (HCC) with congregations stretching from Texas to Georgia, and the Church of the Nazarene, Los Angeles, CA (CN). These three met in Chicago in 1907 and the name Pentecostal Church of the Nazarene was adopted. Two general superintendents, one from the APCA, Hiram Reynolds, and one from the CN, Phineas Bresee, were elected to lead the new church, with E. P. Ellyson from the HCC soon joining them in 1908, marking the official anniversary date of the denomination.

> Perfect love, freed from sin and fear, enables those being made holy to do good to all people.

In 1919 the denomination adopted the official name 'Church of the Nazarene," dropping the word Pentecostal which had been a synonym for holiness in the 19th century but took on new connotations in America with the burgeoning Pentecostal movement after the Azusa Street revival in 1906.[2] Throughout the twentieth century, eight holiness churches and groups would join the original three, marking the Church of the Nazarene as an "ecumenical" merging of churches and groups within the Wesleyan-Holiness tradition.[3]

Several foundational elements have unified the denomination since its inception. A commitment to missions and world-wide holiness ministry was the primary goal of the Church of the Nazarene from its earliest days. Early forms of social ministry appeared in orphanages, hospitals, colleges and schools, and homes for unwed mothers and the poor. Today these ministries continue in areas of anti-human trafficking, refugee work, clean water projects, child sponsorship programs, and in its many graduate seminaries, colleges, and training centers around the world. Revivals and camp meetings provided the primary grounds for evangelism, and a devotion to informal forms of worship

---

2   For a complete history of the Church of the Nazarene, see *Our Watchword and Song,* eds. Stan Ingersol, Floyd Cunningham, and Harold Raser, Kansas City: Nazarene Publishing House, 2013.

3   A chart of the all the groups merging with the Church of the Nazarene in the twentieth century can be found at http://nazarene.org/files/docs/schematic.pdf.

services can be tied to these assemblies. Since 1912, *Holiness Today* (formerly *The Herald of Holiness*) has served as the official magazine of the denomination.

Membership in the church stresses continuing good works in the life of the believer, with an emphasis on ministry to the poor and attention to Christian behavior as seen in the denomination's Covenant of Christian Conduct. The ordination of women and their participation in all areas of church life and leadership has been a continuing hallmark of denominational life, with women being ordained to the ministry since the church's first General Assembly.

Church Structure and Teachings

The polity of the church is structured in a three-tier system at the General, District, and Local levels.[4] At the General and District levels, Superintendents are elected to lead the church in its ministries. The General Assembly meets every four years, elects General Superintendents (currently six in number) and a General Board of international representatives who assist the Superintendents in oversight of the church's work in missions, education, evangelism, and compassion. The General Assembly is composed of representatives from six world areas and serves as the supreme governing body of the denomination, with all of its decisions binding on the church throughout the world. Local churches elect their own pastors in agreement with the District Superintendent, elect their own boards, and oversee ministries in their parish settings.

From its beginning, a Wesleyan *ordo-salutis* or way of salvation has been the central teaching of the Church of the Nazarene. As set forth in its *Manual*, the doctrines of the life of the Trinity, sin, atonement, prevenient grace, justification by faith, the necessity of the sanctification

---

4   The detail is online at http://nazarene.org/files/docs/Manual2013-17.pdf.

of all believers, and the continuing witness to the work of the Holy Spirit in the lives of believers constitute the Nazarene understanding of the way of holiness. This understanding creates a mission that is energized by several core teachings:

1. Salvation and Sanctification are the work of God for all believers, forgiving sin and enabling the believer to a life of love made perfect.

2. An understanding of Scripture as plenary inspired, inerrantly revealing to us all things necessary for our salvation.

3. A life of good works, service, mission, and witness as an expression of God's holy empowerment for living required for all believers.

4. Church membership based on regeneration in the life of the believer.

5. A representative form of church government with both clergy and lay participation.

6. The extension of all forms of ministry and leadership to every believer, including the ordination of women to ministry.

7. A belief in the church as a global entity with a universal polity or governing system for the church world-wide.

Doctrinally, the official creedal statement on holiness for the Church of the Nazarene is found in Article X of its Articles of Faith, entitled *Entire Sanctification*:

> We believe that entire sanctification is that act of God, subsequent to regeneration, by which believers are made free from original sin, or depravity, and brought into a state of entire devotement to God, and the holy obedience of love made perfect.[5]

The love of God defined as "entire devotement to God" and love of neighbor defined as "holy obedience to love made perfect," are both God's work in us and provide the foundation for Nazarene doctrine and Christian living. It is important to note this:

> We believe that the grace of entire sanctification includes the divine impulse to grow in grace as a Christlike disciple. However, this impulse must be consciously nurtured, and careful attention given to the requisites and processes of spiritual development and improvement in Christlikeness of character and personality. Without such purposeful endeavor, one's witness may be impaired and the grace itself frustrated and ultimately lost.[6]

Core Contributions

Central to the story of the Church of the Nazarene is a commitment to John Wesley's ideal of "the world is my parish." Nazarenes have been at the forefront of international efforts of holiness missions since the beginning of the denomination. Further, missionary efforts have always combined evangelism and compassion, linking together as an expression of the holy life the love of God and love of neighbor as the ideal of the sanctified life. Today, Nazarenes serve in 159 countries and

---

5   http://nazarene.org/articles-faith#article-10.

6   http://nazarene.org/articles-faith#article-10.

work with countless international agencies doing good to the bodies and souls of people everywhere. This has been, perhaps, the thing that binds Nazarenes together and has been the one constant unifying element in the church's work throughout its history.

Nazarenes have been ahead of the curve in their commitment to women in ministry. From its beginning it has ordained women to the official ministry of the church and opened the doors for women to be in positions in leadership at every level of church organization. Today, this is a point of concern and struggle for the denomination as well as a guiding light for its future. At one point, as many as twenty percent of its ordained ministers were women, but today that figure has dwindled significantly. However, recent history and the election of the first woman to the General Superintendency in the church, Nina Gunter, shows the continuing commitment of the church to this ideal.

> The ordination of women and their participation in all areas of church leadership have been continuing hallmarks.

The Church of the Nazarene has been especially active in its commitment to an educated ministry, founding and operating numerous educational institutions. Complementing education has been a serious commitment to compassionate ministries, making clear that there is no holiness except social holiness and that the experience of sanctification requires both evangelism and the work of making the world a better and safer place for all people.[7]

Perhaps the greatest challenge to the church, historically and presently, is maintaining a universal church polity or governance structure. The church renewed this commitment with a statement on internationalization in 1980 and created a new administrative strategy by organizing into six world areas, each with the same form and each with a seat at the table of the church's General Assembly. Since then the

---

7   See http://www.ncm.org/ for an exhaustive list of the ministries and agencies the Church of the Nazarene is currently working with.

89

church has elected its first two General Superintendents from outside the United States. The ideals and the theology of the church remain together and significant. Perfect love, freed from sin and fear, found in saints being made holy and doing good to all people in the ministries of the church, continues to energize the efforts of Nazarenes.

CHAPTER 12

THE FREE METHODIST CHURCH

by Howard A. Snyder

The Free Methodist Church was founded in 1860 in the states of New York and Illinois with a vision for renewing and extending the vital mission of early Methodism. Benjamin Titus Roberts (1823-1893), the denomination's principal founder, penned the succinct statement that captures the heart of the church's founding vision. Free Methodists "believe that their mission is twofold – to maintain the Bible standard of Christianity and to preach the Gospel to the poor."

Early Denominational History

American Methodism grew rapidly after 1800. By mid-century it was the largest and most widespread Protestant denomination in the U.S. In the 1840s and 1850s, however, clashing visions of the church's doctrines and mission troubled the Methodist Episcopal Church, particularly in the eastern U.S. Sharp debates emerged in the Genesee Conference in New York.

In 1857 B. T. Roberts, a young Methodist Episcopal pastor in the conference, published the article "New School Methodism," strongly criticizing the growing practice of pew rental in many larger ME churches, the tendency to identify sanctification with justification, and the decline in religious zeal. Roberts said some Methodist preachers were promoting a "new theory of religion" that was "very different from that of the Fathers of Methodism."

Roberts cited two theological errors: putting good works in place of faith in Christ, and holding that justification and sanctification were the same. The "New School Methodists," Roberts said, "depend upon the patronage of the worldly, the favor of the proud and aspiring, and the various artifices of worldly policy." The true mission of Methodism, however, is "not to gather into her fold the proud and fashionable, the devotees of pleasure and ambition, but 'to spread Scriptural holiness over these lands.'"

A dominant group of senior pastors saw Roberts as a trouble-maker. He was tried and reprimanded in 1857, then tried again and expelled from the ME Church in 1858. Unable to regain Methodist membership, Roberts was a freelance evangelist for two years. A series of "Laymen's Conventions" soon led to the formation of the Free Methodist Church in 1860. Roberts was elected the new denomination's first general superintendent.

Revivals led by Methodist lay evangelist John Wesley Redfield (1810-1863) played a role in the denomination's rise. Redfield held revivals in New York, northern Illinois, and in St. Louis, Missouri, which led to early FM churches being organized in those places. Thus, the denomination arose simultaneously in upstate New York, Illinois, and St. Louis – a city where Free Methodist protest against slaveholding was particularly poignant.

With minor exceptions, the Free Methodist Church adopted the doctrines and general structure of the Methodist Episcopal Church. It added an explicit doctrinal article on Entire Sanctification, dropped the title "Bishop," and instituted equal lay and clergy representation at all levels of church government, signaling a more participatory and democratic stance. Its position on the sacraments is essentially that of historic Methodism. The denomination tends to be more liturgical in its sacramental practices than in its general worship patterns, which tend toward an informality influenced by U.S. revivalism.

Expansion and Growth

During its first decades, and especially from 1866 to the early 1890s, the Free Methodist Church showed the character of a *movement*. Growth was fairly rapid as the denomination spread mainly west. By 1890 the church had established twenty-six annual conferences, including one in eastern Canada. Membership rose from about 5,000 in 1866 to 26,000 in 1894, but then slowed. Meanwhile, the denomination launched foreign missions in the 1880s. As growth lessened in North America, it accelerated in places like South Africa, Japan, the Dominican Republic, and later China.[1]

> The mission is twofold—to maintain the Bible standard of Christianity and to preach the gospel to the poor, with the freedom of the Spirit.

The Free Methodist Church grew modestly during what may be called its *sect* phase, from 1890 to about 1950. Focus shifted inward to specifics of behavior and practice rather than outward. Entering the post-World War II boom in the 1950s, the church entered its *denominational* phase, reaching outward in suburban church planting and through the *Light and Life Hour* radio program, increasingly identifying itself as "evangelical," becoming a founding member of the National Association of Evangelicals, and adopting Asbury Theological Seminary as its preferred option for clergy training.

With the larger cultural decline of denominationalism, toward the beginning of the twenty-first century the church became more a loosely-structured *network* than a close-knit "connectional" denomination. By 2014 U.S. membership had reached 73,940. Meanwhile in the 1960s global FM growth surpassed that in North America, and by 2014 world membership stood at 1,128,661, with churches in over eighty nations.

---

1   See Snyder, *Populist Saints*, 667.

In the 1970s Free Methodist world missions pioneered a decentralizing strategy so that by 2015 the denomination had a total of fourteen general conferences, all of equal status, and two "provisional" general conferences expected in time to be full general conferences. This decentralization may be seen as the ongoing fruit of participatory democratic principles introduced at the denomination's founding. A World Conference and other networking structures help provide overall coordination.

Denominational Emphases

With roots in historic Methodism and more remotely the Church of England, the Free Methodist Church stands broadly within the tradition of Christian orthodoxy and Reformed Protestantism. Within this tradition, several emphases are distinctive of the denomination.

1. Holiness. The Free Methodist Church has always been a "holiness denomination" by both tradition and conviction. Doctrinally it has from the first been committed to the Wesleyan doctrine of entire sanctification, though that doctrine has been variously interpreted. For Free Methodists, holiness has meant deep devoutness to God, carefulness and sincerity in personal habits, and high-level commitment to the denomination and one's local congregation. Until the mid-twentieth-century postwar years, most Free Methodists maintained strict standards of simplicity in dress and separation from the world in terms of entertainment. Until the 1950s, Free Methodists were non-instrumental in congregational music, emphasizing vocal and a cappella singing.

2. Racial Justice and Equality. B. T. Roberts and other early Free Methodists opposed slavery and in the U.S. Civil War supported the Union cause. Justice as both a Christian and a civic virtue was deeply embedded in the church's origins and was often stressed in Roberts' writings. The denomination never fully embodied Roberts' ideals in this regard, but this concern for justice has remained a latent impulse throughout history and at different times found expression in the Temperance and anti-secret-society movements. In recent decades the justice concern has been demonstrated in advocacy for the rights of the poor and ethnic minorities and the abolition of sex slavery and exploitation.

3. Full Equality of Women. B. T. and Ellen Roberts and other early Free Methodists championed the full equality of women in home, church, and society. In an early pamphlet Roberts argued for the right of women to preach the gospel. He expanded this in his landmark 1891 book *Ordaining Women.* Although focusing on women's ordination, Roberts argued for the full equality of women in all areas and promoted the idea of marriage as a mutual partnership rather than a hierarchical relationship.

> The church has never been fundamentalistic because of its Methodist roots and their respect for reason and the life of the mind.

It took the denomination until 1974 to fully embrace Roberts' views on ordination. But from the beginning women were prominent in church leadership, particularly as evangelists, church planters, and missionaries. Numerous early FM women leaders specifically cited Roberts' encouragement as key to their own sense of ministry calling.

4. Liberal Arts Orientation. Free Methodists were never fundamentalists because of their rootage in the Methodist tradition with its respect for reason and the life of the mind. As a graduate of Wesleyan University, the flagship Methodist school in Connecticut, Roberts promoted a liberal-arts understanding of life and culture. He founded Chili Seminary (now Roberts Wesleyan College) as a firmly liberal-arts school. This institution in turn became the model for several other FM schools, including (today) Seattle Pacific University, Greenville College, Spring Arbor University, and Central Christian College of Kansas. Another FM school, Los Angeles Pacific College, in 1965 merged with Azusa College to help form what is now Azusa Pacific University.

Throughout its history the denomination experienced some internal tensions between this liberal-arts tradition, carried primarily through its schools, and a more ingrown and somewhat legalistic or fundamentalist orientation found in many local congregations. The denomination experienced some "fundamentalist leavening" in the early 1900s, and from the 1950s on has been influenced somewhat by popular Evangelical dispensationalism and to a lesser degree by Charismatic currents (especially in worship patterns). Yet, officially, it has maintained its Wesleyan-Holiness character, an identity which has received new emphasis and affirmation in the past several decades, including its participation in the Wesleyan Holiness Connection.

5. Global Missions. From the beginning, the Free Methodist Church has been missions-minded. B. T. Roberts considered missionary service in Bulgaria under the ME Church, though he was never appointed. Early Free Methodists had the same missions impulse that marked the ME Church. From the 1880s on, it was active in foreign missionary efforts in China, India, the Dominican Republic, and parts of Africa. The church's continuing missions passion is seen in the increasing growth of global Free Methodism as compared with the denomination's comparatively slow growth in North America.

Contributions to the Holiness Movement and Larger Church

The Free Methodist Church's greatest contribution to the larger church has come through its global missions growth, its educational institutions, and its published authors who are widely read outside the denomination. In terms of theological distinctives, noteworthy are the denomination's emphases on the full equality of women, the freedom of the Spirit, personal holiness, and godly contribution to society. In various times and places these emphases have been muted or compromised, but have functioned as a genetic endowment that periodically reappears with new vigor.

The denomination's strong commitment to liberal arts education, compared with modest numerical growth, means that the church's impact through its educational institutions has been more substantial than its numerical membership would suggest. This liberal-arts orientation characterizes global Free Methodism; several FM colleges, universities, and seminaries have been established in other countries.

Official Denominational Statements

The current (2015) FM *Book of Discipline* carries this declaration:

> *Vision Statement.* To bring wholeness to the world through healthy biblical communities of holy people multiplying disciples, leaders, groups and churches.

The Articles of Religion include this statement entitled "Sanctification," considerably revised from the earlier statement entitled "Entire Sanctification":

> Sanctification is that saving work of God beginning with new life in Christ whereby the Holy Spirit renews His people after the likeness of God, changing them through crisis and process, from one degree of glory to another, and conforming them to the image of Christ.

> As believers surrender to God in faith and die to self through full consecration, the Holy Spirit fills them with love and purifies them from sin. This sanctifying relationship with God remedies the divided mind, redirects the heart to God, and empowers believers to please and serve God in their daily lives.

Thus, God sets His people free to love Him with all their heart, soul, mind, and strength, and to love their neighbor as themselves.[2]

Select Bibliography

Hogue, Wilson T. *History of the Free Methodist Church of North America.* 2 vols. Chicago: Free Methodist Publishing House, 1915.

Lamson, Byron S. *Venture! The Frontiers of Free Methodism.* Winona Lake, Ind.: Light and Life Press, 1960.

Marston, Leslie R. *From Age to Age A Living Witness: A Historical Interpretation of Free Methodism's First Century.* Winona Lake, Ind.: Light and Life Press, 1960.

McKenna, David L. *A Future with a History: The Wesleyan Witness of the Free Methodist Church 1960 to 1995 and Forward.* Indianapolis: Light and Life Communications, 1997.

Snyder, Howard A. *Populist Saints: B. T. and Ellen Roberts and the First Free Methodists.* Grand Rapids: William B. Eerdmans, 2006.

Snyder, Howard A. *Rooted in Mission: The Founding of Seattle Pacific University, 1891-1916.* Seattle: Seattle Pacific University, 2006.

---

2   Free Methodist Church - USA, *2015 Book of Discipline* (Indianapolis: Free Methodist Publishing House, 2016), ¶119.

CHAPTER 13

GRACE COMMUNION INTERNATIONAL

by Joseph Tkach

Herbert W. Armstrong began a radio ministry in the early 1930s that eventually became known as the Radio Church of God and later the Worldwide Church of God (WCG). Armstrong taught numerous unorthodox doctrines, including the seventh-day Sabbath, the annual festivals of Lev. 23, the dietary laws of Lev. 11, an emphasis on millennial prophecy, and a rejection of the Trinity. Although his writings include a few references to salvation by grace, the more common emphasis was that a person must obey God's laws in order for grace to be effective. Sanctification, and hence salvation, was essentially accomplished by works.

After Armstrong died in 1986, the denomination was led by Joseph W. Tkach (1986-1995) and then his son, Joseph Tkach (1995-present). The denomination rejected the unorthodox doctrines and accepted evangelical doctrines, eventually with an emphasis on Trinitarian theology. Membership and income fell dramatically, leading to a thorough restructuring and decentralization. In 2009 the church began using the name Grace Communion International (GCI).[1] There are

---

1   A brief history of these changes is in "Transformed by Christ: A Short History of Grace Communion International," https://www.gci.org/aboutus/history. More details are in J. Michael Feazell, *The Liberation of the Worldwide Church of God* (Zondervan, 2001) and Joseph Tkach, *Transformed by Truth* (Multnomah, 1997).

now about 50,000 members worldwide, meeting in hundreds of small congregations in almost 100 nations.

The connections to the holiness movement are informal. Armstrong came from a Quaker family and his first wife was a Methodist. He was doctrinally eclectic, picking up ideas from various nonconformist movements. The holiness movement played an important role in the denomination's transformation, largely through Azusa Pacific University which was one of the few Christian schools willing to teach WCG leaders. The connections for GCI leadership include:

- Joseph Tkach, GCI President 1996-present (D.Min. APU 2000);

- J. Michael Feazell, GCI Vice President 1999-2012 (D.Min. APU 2001);

- Russell Duke, Grace Communion Seminary President 2003-2016 (Ph.D. Union Institute 1993, professor at APU 1997-present); and

- Michael Morrison, GCS Dean of Faculty 2009-present (M.Div. APU 1997; Ph.D. Fuller Theological Seminary 2006).

Particular Doctrinal Emphases

The doctrines of the Trinity and the Incarnation play prominent roles in the current teachings of Grace Communion International:

- The Father, Son, and Spirit are one God, united in love for one another;

- Jesus Christ, as the Word made flesh, is fully God and fully human;

- Jesus accurately reveals the goodness and love of God, and reveals humanity as God intended us to be;

- As our Creator, Jesus represented all humanity, and all people benefit from his vicarious humanity: his life, death, resurrection and ascension;

- Jesus Christ atoned for all sin and suffered its full consequences;

- God has in Christ reconciled all humanity to himself (however, universal atonement should not be equated with universal salvation);

- The judgment of God against evil has been executed in Jesus Christ so that all might repent and receive forgiveness and, through the Holy Spirit, share in Christ's resurrected, eternal life;

- People are exhorted to respond to this reconciliation and participate in the life for which we were all created; and

- Jesus, as the nexus of divinity and humanity, has enabled humanity to participate in the life and love of the Trinity, which was God's intent from before the beginning of time.[2]

---

2   "Incarnational Trinitarian Theology: A Brief Outline," https://www.gci.org/aboutus/theology. A longer outline is at "An Introduction to Trinitarian Theology," https://www.gci.org/theology.

The vicarious humanity of Jesus Christ is crucial for our holiness. Humans are holy only by being united to Christ. He defines humanity, and he defines holiness. Our attempts at holiness always fall short; it is only through his holiness that we can be holy. Just as he cleansed lepers by touching them, he has cleansed humanity by taking humanity into himself. Humans are set apart for his use, and we live holy lives not to earn his favor but because he has already given us his favor. Holiness is expressed as the Spirit lives in us, leading us to a Christ-like life.[3]

Contributions

Grace Communion International is small in size and young in orthodoxy, but it does have a few things that may be of value to the larger Christian community:

1. The history of transformation from legalism to grace. Herbert Armstrong was not the only teacher, nor was WCG the only denomination in which the desire to obey God turned into legalism. Many people are attracted to legalism; they like to think that their performance adds at least a little to their salvation. A more accurate analogy might be that obedience in faith is merely a sign that we enjoy what Christ has given. Our enjoyment has no merit of its own, and our obedience always falls short of the ideal.

2. GCI's history has forced the denomination to renounce legalistic approaches to holiness and ethics, and to stress the efficacy of grace. But grace is not license to sin, nor does it do away with guidance given

---

3   For an article about sanctification, see "Sanctification," https://www.gci.org/gospel/sanctification.

to us in Scripture about how a Christian is to live. Christ died for us while we were sinners, even before we were alive. Grace always comes first. Obedience must be seen as a response to grace, rather than as a way to earn it.

3. Even our best efforts fall short of the ideal; we must always rely on the merits of Christ from start to finish. Our lives are hidden in him (Colossians 3:3); he is our righteousness, our sanctification, and our salvation (1 Corinthians 1:30). As the representative for all humanity, Jesus offered to God the perfect obedience that we all need. It is only through him that we can be completely holy.

4. Jesus died for all humanity; the payment has already been given for all sins – past, present and future. In Christ, God has reconciled the world to himself (Colossians 1:20), not counting their sins against them (2 Corinthians 5:19; Colossians 2:14). Forgiveness has already been given, but not everyone has learned of it or accepted it. Lamentably, it seems that some will reject it. Christ has brought them to the celebration, but they refuse to go in (cf. Luke 15:28). He gives them a ticket to an eternity of love, joy and peace, but they do not want salvation on the terms that he gives.

> Jesus, the nexus of divinity and humanity, enables humanity to participate in the life and love of the Trinity.

5. The denominational history forced GCI to grapple with numerous doctrines. After the faulty doctrinal

edifice of Herbert W. Armstrong collapsed, church leaders searched for a biblical way to connect the various doctrines again. Incarnational Trinitarian theology provided a useful framework that coheres with Scripture and church history. GCI now offers a website with thousands of articles about Christian theology, the Bible, ministry, and Christian life.[4] Also on the website are more than 120 interviews with Trinitarian theologians from several denominations.

6. Most GCI congregations have bivocational pastors. To help train these leaders without removing them from their ministries, GCI developed Grace Communion Seminary, which offers accredited master's degrees with all work done online. The courses and the cost are designed for part-time students; full-time students are also welcome.[5]

Official Statements Related to Holiness

The Grace Communion International *Statement of Beliefs* says:

Christian conduct is characterized by trust in and loving allegiance to Jesus Christ, who loved us and gave himself for us. Trust in Jesus Christ is expressed by belief in the gospel and by participation in Jesus Christ's works of love. Through the Holy Spirit, Christ transforms the hearts of

---

4   For theology, see https://www.gci.org/theology/articles. For the Bible, see https://www.gci.org/bible. For ministry, https://www.gci.org/church. For Christian life, https://www.gci.org/disc/misc.

5   See www.gcs.edu. The Seminary is accredited by the Distance Education Accrediting Commission, an agency recognized by the U.S. Department of Education and the Council for Higher Education Accreditation.

believers, producing in them love, joy, peace, faithfulness, meekness, kindness, goodness, gentleness, self-control, righteousness, and truth.[6]

A denominational article about sanctification states:

> God sets people apart as "holy" for the purpose that they live holy lives in following Jesus Christ. We are saved so that we might produce good works and good fruit (Ephesians 2:8-10; Galatians 5:22-23). The good works are not a cause of salvation, but a result of it. Good works are evidence that a person's faith is genuine (James 2:18). Paul speaks of the "obedience of faith" and says that faith expresses itself in love (Romans 1:5; Galatians 5:6).[7]

From the article "An Introduction to Trinitarian Theology":

> God is not just giving us existence that lasts forever – he is giving us life of a certain *quality*, life that is based on love rather than selfishness and competition. That's the kind of life we will enjoy in eternity, and that's the kind of life that is *good*, not just in the future but also right now. When the New Testament gives us commands, it is describing for us the kind of life that God is giving us, the life of the age to come. Grace says: I am giving you a never-ending life of joy. The commands say: This is what it looks like. This is the way that will help you have joy and express love . . . .

> Humans are holy by being united to Christ. Holiness is expressed as the Spirit lives in us.

---

6   Quoted from "Statement of Beliefs," www.gci.org/aboutus/beliefs.

7   Michael Morrison, "Sanctification," https://www.gci.org/gospel/sanctification.

A Trinitarian understanding of our purpose in life helps us see the purpose of salvation, and the purpose of the commands we see in the Bible. Once we see where we are going, it is easier to see how God is bringing us there. Love is central to the whole picture, because love is the life of the Father, Son and Spirit, and we are participating in the divine nature, sharing in the life and love of the Triune God.

As images of God, we want our life to be characteristic of the age to come, patterned after the life that God himself has. We are images of God and representatives of God, and we should want to live in the way that he does. This life is representative of God himself, a fulfillment of the image that we are supposed to be. And in the age to come, we will forever be images of God, children of God, completely and perfectly.[8]

---

8   https://www.gci.org/intro.

THE INTERNATIONAL PENTECOSTAL HOLINESS CHURCH

by A. D. Beacham, Jr.

The International Pentecostal Holiness Church (IPHC) traces its organizational roots to 1898 and its theological/ecclesiastical roots to John Wesley, Methodism in the United States, and some aspects of the Thirty-Nine Articles of the Church of England.[1]

Historical Origins

The early leaders of IPHC came from the broad stream of the late nineteenth-century holiness revival. That revival laid the foundation for the emergence of numerous holiness denominations, including the Christian and Missionary Alliance, the Church of the Nazarene, and the Church of God (Cleveland, Tennessee), one of the Wesleyan holiness churches that became Pentecostal following Azusa Street in 1906.[2] Most of the early IPHC leaders were reared in Methodist congregations

---

1   IPHC goes by IPHC Ministries and the official web page is www.iphc.org.

2   See Vinson Synan's definitive *The Holiness-Pentecostal Movement in the United States* (Wm. B. Eerdmans, 1971) for a description of these movements and how they were antecedents to several Pentecostal groups in the United States.

prior to leaving that movement during the holiness controversies of the 1890s.

The decade of the 1890s saw the emergence of two small holiness groups that later merged to form the IPHC. One was the *Fire-Baptized Holiness Church* (FBHC) founded by Benjamin H. Irwin. Irwin's work, which developed extreme views even by holiness standards, grew initially in the mid-western United States and expanded to southern states. It was autocratic and through Irwin's influence developed a series of emotionally expressed religious experiences. It was formally established in 1898 in Anderson, South Carolina, but soon Irwin confessed to moral failure and left the movement.

The movement staggered at the news of Irwin's fall and almost totally collapsed. It took the efforts of a young Joseph H. King to hold it together and bring about theological and ecclesiastical order. King, who was in his early thirties at this time, was living in rural north Georgia. Earlier King had attended seminary at the U. S. Grant University in Chattanooga, Tennessee (now University of Tennessee Chattanooga) and became a minister in the Methodist Church, North serving congregations in North Georgia.

> The IPHC is rooted firmly in the Lutheran Reformation and the Wesleyan and Azusa Pentecostal revivals.

The core theology of this group was Wesleyan, featuring justification by faith, sanctification as a second work of grace, divine healing, and the second coming of Jesus. Like most other holiness groups at that time, the baptism in the Holy Spirit was considered to be synonymous with sanctification.

There are several contributions from the FBHC that should be remembered. First, Irwin's movement spread across the United States from Kansas and Oklahoma to the south and also to the north and into Canada. Second, Irwin helped lay the foundation for a distinction between the baptism in the Holy Spirit and sanctification. Third, Irwin's and King's ministries left a printed legacy in a publication named *Live Coals of Fire* that later became *Live Coals*.

The second group was located primarily in eastern North Carolina. Called the Holiness Church of North Carolina,[3] it was established by Methodist minister A. B. Crumpler. In the 1890s Crumpler began preaching holiness and by 1896 was in serious conflict with local Methodist leaders. By 1898 he withdrew from the Methodist church and formed the first Pentecostal Holiness Church in Goldsboro, North Carolina. That congregation continues to this day as a thriving ministry serving Goldsboro and eastern North Carolina. The two groups knew one another's leaders as they traveled across the southeast preaching at camp meetings. They also recognized one another from the holiness magazines produced by the two groups and by others.

Both groups were significantly impacted by the Azusa Street revival in Los Angeles in April, 1906. A member of the Holiness Church of North Carolina, Gaston Barnabas Cashwell, traveled to Los Angeles in November, 1906, to learn more of the revival sweeping the world. Cashwell received the Pentecostal experience of speaking in other tongues and adopted the Azusa theological construct of Pentecost as a third spiritual experience distinct from sanctification. He returned to Dunn, North Carolina, in early December and began a "Pentecostal" revival there on December 31. That revival continued into January and over the next two years spread to both the Fire-Baptized Holiness Church and the Pentecostal Holiness Church of North Carolina.

The two groups, with similar theologies, merged in Falcon, North Carolina, on January 31, 1911, and formed the foundation of the Pentecostal Holiness Church.[4]

---

3   The Holiness Church of North Carolina was also known as the Pentecostal Holiness Church of North Carolina prior to 1906. This was because, prior to Azusa Street, "Pentecostal" and "sanctification" were considered the same.

4   More historical information can be found in Vinson Synan, "The Old-Time Power" (Advocate Press: Franklin Springs, GA, 1973); A. D. Beacham, Jr., "A Brief History of the Pentecostal Holiness Church" (Advocate Press: Franklin Springs, GA, 1990); and Beacham, "Azusa East: The Life and Times of G. B. Cashwell" (LSR Publications: Franklin Springs, GA, 2006).

Theological Foundations

The IPHC is rooted firmly in three significant moves of God. First, the church is rooted in the Lutheran Reformation with its emphases on justification by faith, the authority of Scripture, and the universal priesthood of all believers. Second, it is rooted in the Wesleyan revival in England. Third, it is rooted in the Azusa Pentecostal revival. The theological emphasis of the denomination is reflected in its name: Pentecost and Holiness.

The church affirms the historic creeds of Christendom: Apostles' Creed and the Nicene Creed. Other aspects of historic Christianity affirmed through the seven major church councils are recognized by the denomination. We intentionally added to our doctrinal statements emphases on the nature of God (the Trinity, Jesus Christ) and Articles of Faith taken from the Thirty-Nine Articles of the Church of England. This connection is due to the influence of Wesley and Methodism.

For the average member of the denomination, theology is expressed in five statements: we believe in justification by faith through Jesus Christ; we believe in sanctification as a second definite work of grace; we believe in the baptism in the Holy Spirit with the initial evidence of speaking in other tongues; we believe in divine healing as provided in the atonement; and we believe in the personal, premillennial, second coming of Jesus Christ.

Ecclesiastical Structures and Core Values

The IPHC Vision is reflected in two statements expressing Isaiah 54:2-3. IPHC is "A Place of Hope, A People of Promise." The mission statement is "The mission of the International Pentecostal Holiness Church is to multiply believers and churches, discipling them in worship, fellowship, and evangelism as we obey the Great Commission in cooperation with the whole body of Christ."

The Core Values are: We Prayerfully Value Scripture; We Prayerfully Value Pentecost; We Prayerfully Value Holiness; We Prayerfully

Value Christ's Kingdom; We Prayerfully Value Every Generation; We Prayerfully Value Justice; and We Prayerfully Value Generosity. IPHC ordains women as ministers and they may serve in any capacity in the denomination. Most of our social issue stances are reflected in the position papers of the National Association of Evangelicals. The denomination is solidly pro-life and affirming marriage only between a man and woman.

The influence of Methodism is reflected in our use of conferences as judicatories. The leader of these judicatories is called "Bishop" and holds the office of the Conference Superintendent. Currently there are thirty conferences in the United States. Every four years the IPHC holds a General Conference. While most of the delegates are from the USA, many of our 100 plus nations with an IPHC ministry presence are represented. The leadership of the denomination is elected at the General Conference. There currently are four persons, the General Superintendent (Presiding Bishop), the Executive Director of Discipleship Ministries, the Executive Director of Evangelism USA, and the Executive Director of World Missions Ministries. Each of these executives serves as a general bishop in IPHC. These bishops relate to the Council of Bishops composed of the conference superintendents in the USA.

> We prayerfully value Scripture, Pentecost, Holiness, Christ's Kingdom, Justice, and Generosity.

IPHC has three higher education entities in the United States: Emmanuel College (Franklin Springs, Georgia), Southwestern Christian University (Oklahoma City, Oklahoma), and Advantage College (California). Holmes Bible College in Greenville, South Carolina, has a long and fruitful ministry with the IPHC. There are over thirty Bible schools outside the USA. Falcon Children's Home in Falcon, North Carolina, provides care for children and unwed mothers as an alternative to abortion. The Children's Center Hospital in Bethany, Oklahoma, has a long history with IPHC support, and the Executive Committee serves as the Trustees of this outstanding medical facility.

Relationships with Other Christians and the WHC

As reflected in the close of the mission statement, we seek to serve "in cooperation with the whole body of Christ." IPHC was a founding member of the National Association of Evangelicals, Pentecostal and Charismatic Churches of North America, and Christian Churches Together. We are also active with Empowered 21 and the Billion Soul Campaign. IPHC leaders and scholars also have participated in various ways with the Wesleyan Holiness Connection and continue to support its goals and affirmations for the churches of our generation.

CHAPTER 15

INTERNATIONAL CHURCH OF THE FOURSQUARE GOSPEL

by Jack W. Hayford

The International Church of the Foursquare Gospel is a Pentecostal church that was founded in the 1920s and based in Los Angeles, California. Because of its beginnings as the outgrowth of dynamic evangelistic ministry, its early constituents came from many different churches and backgrounds, many from the Azusa Street revival.

Brief History

The International Church of the Foursquare Gospel, also known as The Foursquare Church, developed out of the ministry of the dynamic evangelist Aimee Semple McPherson, who opened Angelus Temple in Los Angeles on January 1, 1923. Because of the founder's commitment to worldwide and interdenominational evangelism (as noted on the cornerstone of Angelus Temple), the church attracted people from many different religious backgrounds, cultures, and ethnicities.

Sister McPherson, who was born again under the ministry of Robert Semple (whom she later married), had a mixed religious heritage. Her father was a Methodist and her mother belonged to the Salvation Army. Robert Semple was greatly influenced by the Azusa

Street Revival and, after they were married, Robert and Aimee Semple worked with evangelist W. H. Durham in Chicago (McPherson 1923). Those three streams of religious practice helped shape the denomination that arose from Sister McPherson's ministry.

Robert and Aimee Semple went as missionaries to China when Aimee was not even twenty years old. Robert died after only a few months, and Aimee returned to the U.S. with a newborn daughter and little else. But the evangelistic zeal that had compelled her to go to the far ends of the earth never left her. After traveling as an evangelist for several years, Aimee Semple McPherson opened Angelus Temple, not thinking that it would be the beginning of the International Church of the Foursquare Gospel. What began as one church in the early 20th century has extended now in the 21st to a constituency of almost nine million believers in 149 countries and territories.

> Aimee Semple McPherson directed a diversity of people to the cause of interdenominational and worldwide evangelism.

Central Teachings

The church's four cardinal doctrines, as well as the church's name, derived from a sermon Sister McPherson preached in Oakland, California, in 1922 – a message based on a vision of Ezekiel. The following is taken from that sermon, which was printed in its entirety in *The Bridal Call* in January, 1923:

> "And I looked, and, behold, a whirlwind came out of the North, a great cloud, and a fire infolding itself, and a brightness was about it, and out of the midst thereof as the color of amber, out of the midst of the fire. Also out of the midst thereof came the likeness of four living creatures. And this was their appearance; they had the likeness of a man. And

as for the likeness of their faces, they four had the face of a man, and the face of a lion, on the right side: and they four had the face of an ox on the left side; they four also had the face of an eagle" (Ezekiel 1:4, 5 and 10).

And from out of the midst thereof – out of the midst of the cloud of Grace – there comes the four-square Gospel of our Lord and Saviour Jesus Christ, as four living creatures, having the likeness of a Man. What a glorious gospel it is, with straight feet sparkling like burnished brass, and with rushing, mighty, tender feathered wings that turn not as they go but bear "straight forward" the glory and the majesty of the great Jehovah Jirah! As these were "living creatures" so is the gospel living, moving, vitally alive. The Gospel which is borne to us is indeed a four-square Gospel, facing the world four-square, revealing four different faces or phases of the Gospel, all of which bear faithful likeness to the man Jesus Christ.

- The face of the man: Jesus Christ, the only Saviour.

- The face of the lion: Jesus Christ, the baptizer with the Holy Ghost.

- The face of the ox: Jesus Christ, the great physician.

- The face of the eagle: Jesus Christ, the coming king.

Church Statements Regarding Holy Living

The Foursquare Church has a "Declaration of Faith" which articulates its primary doctrines and the supporting scriptures for them. Article VIII states the following:

We believe that having been cleansed by the precious blood of Jesus Christ and having received the witness of the Holy Spirit at conversion, it is the will of God that we be sanctified daily and become partakers of His holiness; growing constantly stronger in faith, power, prayer, love and service, first as babies desiring the sincere milk of the Word; then as dear children walking humbly, seeking diligently the hidden life, where self decreases and Christ increases; then as strong men having on the whole armor of God, marching forth to new conquests in His name beneath His blood-stained banner, ever living a patient, sober, unselfish, godly life that will be a true reflection of the Christ within.

Founder Aimee Semple McPherson also compiled a document containing forty creedal statements. Of those, four (25-28) specifically relate to the call to holy living:

We believe: In the maintenance of good works and holy living.

We believe: In the victorious life over sin, self, and bad habits by Bible study and an incessant prayer life.

We believe: In Christian perfection and holiness, through absolute surrender and consecration.

We believe: In Christian modesty in the matter of dress, wearing apparel, and jewelry. It should be noted that the context of holiness and sanctification is in the totality of a life lived for God's glory, surrendered to His will and committed to advancing His Kingdom.

Core Contributions

In order to understand the contributions of The Foursquare Church it is important to note that its mission statement is contained on the cornerstone of its flagship church, Angelus Temple:

> Dedicated unto the Cause of Interdenominational and Worldwide Evangelism

Only four years after the founding of Angelus Temple, Sister McPherson sent missionaries to the Philippines. The good news was not something to be received and enjoyed in the comforts of home; people all over the world were entitled to hear the gospel. People were encouraged to go or to give so that others could go. That "sending" emphasis as a personal response to having received the gospel has greatly influenced many in the larger body of Christ.

> Being cleansed by the blood of Jesus Christ, we are to be sanctified daily, becoming partakers of God's holiness.

The cornerstone also includes the term "interdenominational." Sister McPherson, who had no intention to start a denomination when she opened Angelus Temple as a revival center, respected and fellowshipped with people from various churches and denominations. That is a trait that still distinguishes The Foursquare Church today. In fact, creedal statements 39 and 40 state the following:

> We believe: In Christian tolerance of all denominations of the Christian faith.

> We believe: In essentials – unity; in non-essentials – liberty; in all things – charity.

Another distinct contribution of The Foursquare Church is its emphasis on moderation. In fact, that trait is addressed in article XIII of Foursquare's Declaration of Faith:

> We believe that the moderation of the believer should be known of all men; that his experience and daily walk should never lead him into extremes, fanaticism, unseemly manifestations, back-bitings, murmurings; but that his sober, thoughtful, balanced, mellow, forgiving, and zealous Christian experience should be one of steadfast uprightness, equilibrium, humility, self-sacrifice and Christ-likeness.

It is this commitment to moderation that has kept the church from embracing practices and ideologies that have proven destructive throughout the years.

In an ever-shrinking world that is increasingly divided along ethnic, cultural and racial boundaries, The Foursquare Church's emphasis on sharing the gospel with every person in every part of the world is an important reminder that the scope of the Great Commission is both interdenominational and worldwide. The church must be steadfast in sharing the gospel and making disciples, teaching people to pursue lives of godly moderation and holiness, and ensuring that the disciple-making process is infinitely reproducible.

The Foursquare Church is convinced that the Spirit of God continues to work in our time for the sake of Christian holiness in the churches and individual believers. It is privileged to participate with the Wesleyan Holiness Connection in being a catalyst for this ongoing revival. The Church is pleased that one of its own contemporary leaders, Rev. Kimberly Dirmann, is providing vital leadership as a member of the Board of Directors of the Connection.

Select Bibliography

McPherson, Aimee Semple. "Declaration of Faith."

McPherson, Aimee Semple. "Creedal Statements."

McPherson, Aimee Semple. *The Bridal Call*. January 1923.

McPherson, Aimee Semple. *The Collected Sermons and Writings of Aimee Semple McPherson*. Vols. 1-3. Los Angles: Echo Park Evangelistic Association, 2015.

McPherson, Aimee Semple. *This Is That*. Los Angeles: Echo Park Evangelistic Association, 1923.

CHAPTER 16

THE SALVATION ARMY

by Jonathan S. Raymond

Since its inception in 1865, The Salvation Army's (TSA) roots go deeply into the soil of the Wesleyan holiness movement. The co-founders, William and Catherine Booth, were thoroughly Wesleyan in their theological views and practices.

William Booth joined the Methodist New Connection in 1850. He was an ordained Methodist minister (1858). When he left the New Connection in 1862, he appropriated their doctrines, including the wording of the eighth doctrine: "It is our privilege to be fully sanctified in the name of the Lord Jesus Christ, and by the Spirit of our God." Those words framed the future of TSA distinctly within a Wesleyan holiness context.

Grounded in Wesleyan Theology

TSA began as a ministry to the poor in East London under another name, The Christian Mission. TSA continued its doctrinal grounding in Wesleyan theology, articulating basic Methodist orthodoxy in its own language. Two articles of faith out of eleven were focused on the process and crisis of holiness:

> 9. *We believe that continuance in a state of salvation depends upon continued obedient faith in Christ.*

By "state of salvation" TSA affirms a Wesleyan full salvation "from the uttermost of sin and death to the uttermost of holiness and infilling by the Spirit of God. By "state" TSA means a dynamic, interactive, synergistic relationship with Christ in the context of sustained obedient faith. As an ongoing process, Salvationists believe that our salvation is our restoration by God to the *Imago Dei*. In this sense, we are daily "being saved" (Acts 2:47), continually restored in the process of being perfected.

> 10. *We believe that it is the privilege of all believers to be wholly sanctified, and that their whole spirit, soul and body may be preserved blameless unto the coming of our Lord Jesus Christ.*

By "wholly sanctified" TSA affirms the doctrine of entire sanctification in this life. John Wesley's continuum of grace (the *Via Salutis*: prevenient, justifying, sanctifying, and glorifying grace) articulates the progress of a Christ follower in the likeness of Jesus Christ, and the infilling of God's Holy Spirit that occasions purity of heart and life.

Struggling to Stay Balanced

Historically, like much of the Wesleyan holiness movement in general, TSA was influenced by nineteenth-century American revivalists. William and Catherine Booth were highly influenced by the evangelical orientations of Asa Mahan and Charles Finney. The preaching and personal friendships of Phoebe Palmer and James Caughey helped to steer the TSA's holiness trajectory away from a more balanced expression of Wesleyan theology and practice. They occasioned in the Booths an "Americanesque" evangelical impulse for a fast track crisis experience of holiness at the alter in the context of revival enthusiasm. In the early years, the Booths believed that the Lord Jesus was returning at any moment and that their work was to save as many souls and sanctify as many saints as quickly as possible. The quick, new orientations of the American style, crisis-oriented sanctification fit the missional vision of the Booths at the time.

It wasn't until Samuel Logan Brengle (1860-1936) came on the scene that the TSA began to adjust back to more balanced thinking and practice in line with the original orthodoxy and orthopraxy of Wesleyan holiness. Brengle stated clearly that holiness was both process and crisis. TSA doctrines already supported the idea of growth in grace toward increasing Christ-likeness (process) through its doctrine nine, but it was Brengle's writings that provided ballast for TSA's doctrinal ship of holiness.

Subsequently, Gunpei Yamamuro, Frederick Coutts, Milton Agnew, Edward Read, and many contemporary TSA authors have contributed to a balanced discussion of holiness within TSA. After 150 years of mission and ministry, TSA remains faithful to its central tenet of a full and free salvation by grace through faith, and its doctrines of initial, synergistic (progressive), and entire sanctification.

> It is the privilege of all believers to be wholly sanctified, changed into the likeness of Jesus Christ by the infilling of God's Holy Spirit.

Enriching the Whole Church

From its early beginnings to the present day the ethos of TSA has been the Wesleyan idea of inward and outward holiness. The Booths embraced Wesley's conjunctive idea of holiness of both heart and life. Out of the Spirit-filled essence of TSA, it offers the larger Christian community and the world a balanced approach to mission and ministry. Out of a compellingly profound love of God and others, TSA strives to be faithful to its seminal purpose: to save souls, grow saints, and serve suffering humanity.

In growing saints (making disciples) the holiness catechesis of TSA emphasizes a balanced integration of knowing Christ (orthodoxy), loving Christ (cardio-pathy), and living Christ (orthopraxy). Out of that orientation, Salvationist ministry is characterized by knowing, loving, and living for others personally in inward holiness and socially in outward holiness. In faithfulness to a Wesleyan framework of ministry and mission, TSA is characterized by the divine means of grace reflected in acts of piety and mercy in obedience to our Lord's Great Commandment and Great Commission.

TSA is 150 years old at this writing. That is only 7% of the 2,000-year history of the church. Such accounting occasions humility and respect for the saints that preceded it, for the long history of others in the body of Christ. Nevertheless, in its brief history the Salvation Army as a missional movement has been blessed to be a blessing in many parts of the world. Today TSA embraces Wesley's vision to "spread scriptural holiness throughout the land" in 127 countries from Angola and Zimbabwe to Fiji, The Faefos, and Finland. TSA is relatively small with 13,000 churches (corps), 26,881 officers (clergy), 11,664 employees, and 1.4 million soldiers (members).

Serving Suffering Humanity

TSA is best known for serving suffering humanity. It does so through the ministry of residential hostels for the homeless, emergency lodges, children's homes, homes for the elderly, disabled, blind, street children, abandoned babies, residential care homes/hostels, day care centers, residential and non-residential addiction programs, Harbor Light centers for alcohol recovery, services to the armed forces, emergency disaster response programs, prison ministries, missing person services, employment bureau, emergency relief (fire, flood, etc.), hostels for students, general hospitals, hospice centers, health education programs, community centers, and over 3,000 schools (primary, kindergarten, middle, secondary, vocational), colleges and universities.

The global extent of TSA's programs and social services relative to its size is a reality only explained as the grace of God. TSA's collective flaws, shortcomings, human failings, and weaknesses are an accompanying reality. Nevertheless, God's grace is sufficient and his power is made perfect in weakness. TSA's steadfast pursuit of personal, social, and corporate holiness as one Army, with one worldwide mission, serving one God, occasions God's faithfulness in producing the fruit of TSA's social services to the glory of God.

> The Army strives to be faithful to its seminal purpose: to save souls, grow saints, and serve suffering humanity.

God's empowerment of the TSA to serve suffering humanity is a testimony to the larger Christian community. God is faithful and his grace is sufficient. Holiness within TSA is at the heart of God's blessing as he does immeasurably more that we could ask or imagine. The TSA responds in sanctified worship to God and in serving others expressly to the praise of God's glory.

The overarching idea of holiness within TSA is the whole person being redirected toward the highest spiritual end. That end is the fullness of God in the likeness of Christ to the glory of God. Inward holiness for Salvationists is a matter of purity of heart and profound love of God. Outward holiness is most clearly revealed in Salvationist's profound love of God evident in thanks and praise and in a profound, love of others in sacrificial service. Glory to God!

There is no such thing as holiness apart from "Christ in you."
— Samuel Logan Brengle

Select Bibliography

The Salvation Army has a long history of authors on the topic of holiness from a Wesleyan-Holiness perspective. However, Army holiness authors and literature are not well known because of a history of the Army publishing works in house and expressly for Salvationists. Nevertheless, following are a few of the Army's classics on the topic of holiness.

Bob Hostetler (editor), *Samuel L. Brengle's Holy Life Series*, Wesleyan Publishing House and Crest Books, 2016. Includes Brengle's six holiness classics: *Helps to Holiness, The Heart of Holiness, Ancient Prophets and Modern Problems, The Servant's Heart, Resurrection Life and Power,* and *Come Holy Guest.* Other books by Samuel L. Brengle on holiness include *The Way of Holiness, Heart Talks on Holiness,* and *Take Time to be Holy.*

Frederick Coutts. *The Call to Holiness.* London: Salvationist Publishing, 1964.

Frederick Coutts. *The Splendour of Holiness.* London: Salvationist Publishing, 1983.

Amy Reardon, *Holiness Revealed: A Devotional Study in Hebrews.* Wesleyan Publishing House and Crest Books, 2015.

Word & Deed: The Salvation Army Journal of Theology and Ministry, Roger J. Green and Jonathan S. Raymond (Co-Editors), 1998 to the present. Contains several articles on holiness by contemporary Salvationist authors.

CHAPTER 17

THE UNITED METHODIST CHURCH

by Laurence W. Wood

John Wesley said that "God raised up the people called Methodists to spread Scriptural holiness across these lands."[1] This chapter explains the original vision of John and Charles Wesley and how the United Methodist Church has sought to implement it over the generations.

Beginnings with the Wesleys

After completing his B.A. degree in 1725 at the age of twenty-two, John Wesley was made a deacon in Christ Church Cathedral. Then he was elected a fellow and tutor of Lincoln College, Oxford University. Meanwhile, his younger brother Charles began to meet with some of his fellow students at Oxford for the purpose of pursuing the holy life. John joined this group and organized it into what was called "The Holy Club." Its purpose was to study together (especially the Scriptures), engage in rigorous spiritual self-examination, and participate in works of charity. In 1732 the critics called the Club "Methodists." The Wesley brothers sailed to America in 1735 to become missionaries and cultivate

---

1   "Minutes of Several Conversations" Q.3 *Works of John Wesley.* ed. T. Jackson (Baker Book House, 1978), 8:299. http://www.umc.org/how-we-serve/vital-congregations-our-legacy.

the sense of holiness in their lives, but they soon returned, feeling defeated in their mission.

Their pursuit would continue, with the three primary influences on the Wesley brothers being William Law, Peter Böhler, and Christian David. First, they read Law's *A Practical Treatise upon Christian Perfection* (1726). Law became their mentor. His mysticism entailed the idea of becoming holy through spiritual disciplines such as self-denial, engaging in works of charity, and participating in the ordinances of the Church of England. The activities in the Holy Club were designed to implement the disciplines prescribed by Law. John Wesley preached "The Circumcision of Heart" in 1733, virtually a mirror image of ideas found in William Law's book.

In 1738 the Wesleys met Peter Böhler and for the first time heard that saving faith is attained instantaneously through being justified by faith alone. John reviewed the conversion accounts in the book of Acts and was led to accept Böhler's Moravian teaching. On May 21 and May 28, 1738, Charles and John respectively experienced their evangelical conversions. Because they had equated Law's idea of perfection with Böhler's idea of justification by faith, John believed that he had attained Christian perfection: "I have *constant peace*; – not one uneasy thought. And I have *freedom from sin*; – not one unholy desire."[2] Very soon, however, he realized that he was still experiencing doubt and fear and lacked the full assurance of faith. This confusion prompted him to visit Herrnhut, Germany, the headquarters of the Moravian community so that "those holy men . . . would be a means, under God, of so establishing my soul."[3]

The most significant person met there by John Wesley was one of the original leaders of the Moravian community at Herrnhut,

---

2   John Wesley, May 29, 1738, *Journals and Diaries I (1735-38)*, ed. W. Reginald Ward and Richard Heitzenrater, 18:253.

3   John Wesley, June 7-June 13, 1738, *Journals and Diaries I (1735-38)*, ed. W. Reginald Ward and Richard Heitzenrater, 18:254.

THE UNITED METHODIST CHURCH • 129

Christian David. This contact profoundly influenced John.[4] This lay preacher explained that there is a time difference in the experience of justifying faith and the full assurance of faith (being cleansed from all sin). This temporal distinction was explained as corresponding to the justifying faith of the disciples before Pentecost and the full cleansing and assurance of faith on the day of Pentecost. John used this pattern of the disciples' experience of justification and full sanctification as a basis for interpreting his own experience of Aldersgate.

> John Wesley said that "God raised up the people called Methodists to spread Scriptural holiness across these lands."

This use can be seen in the September, 16, 1738, letter to his older brother Samuel, written one month after his return from Herrnhut to England, and in the 1739 volume *Hymns and Sacred Poems* published jointly by John and Charles. Soon they said that they did not know a single instance of a person's receiving, *in one and the same moment*, remission of sins and the abiding witness of the Spirit, which includes a new, a clean heart.[5]

In 1760, John Wesley began to make some modifications in his understanding, as it can be seen in his sermon on "The New Birth."[6] Previously he had made a distinction between being born of God in the imperfect sense and being born of God in the larger sense of full sanctification. Whereas earlier he had defined Christian perfection in terms of the indwelling of the Spirit,[7] in his sermon on "Sin in Believers" he acknowledged that every justified believer has the indwelling of the

---

4   Ward and Heitzenrater, *Journals and Diaries II*, 18:273n.

5   John Wesley, "Preface," *Hymns and Sacred Poems* (1740), *Doctrinal and Controversial Treatises II*, eds. Paul Wesley Chilcote and Kenneth J. Collins, *The Bicentennial Edition of the Works of John Wesley* (Nashville: Abingdon Press, 2013): 13:46.

6   Albert Outler, *Sermons*, 2:186, "The New Birth."

7   *John Wesley,* "The Principles of a Methodist" (1742), in *The Methodist Societies: History, Nature, and Design,* ed. Rupert E. Davies, Wesley, *Works*, 9:64-65.

Spirit.[8] Another shift was his idea of the meaning of "full assurance of faith."　　.

The Methodist Tradition Over Time

The Methodist Episcopal Church was officially authorized to become a new denomination at the Baltimore Christmas Conference in 1784, after John Wesley had ordained Thomas Coke to come to America with the instruction to ordain Francis Asbury and for both Asbury and Coke to become the first two general superintendents (bishops). The Methodist Episcopal Church soon became the largest Protestant denomination in the United States, and now is the second largest next to the Southern Baptist Convention.

Dr. Glen Alton Messer, II, in his 2006 dissertation titled *Restless for Zion, New England Methodism, Holiness, and the Abolitionist Struggle, Circa 1789-1845*, traced the introduction of Methodism into the New England region and traced the influences of the Christian perfection doctrine on mission efforts, education, and the anti-slavery movement. The Methodist Episcopal Church, South, and the Methodist Protestant Church merged with the Methodist Episcopal Church in 1939 to form the Methodist Church. In 1968 it merged with the Evangelical United Brethren Church to form the present United Methodist Church.

John Fletcher wrote his defense of the theology of John Wesley in his *Checks to Antinomianism*, and his writings became recognized as authoritative and were required reading in the ministerial course of study of all Methodist ministers.[9] However, toward the second half of the nineteenth century theological liberalism began to characterize the Methodist Episcopal Church and the Wesleyan Holiness Movement

8   Albert Outler, *Sermons*, 1:328, "On Sin in Believers."

9   Randy L. Maddox, "Respected Founder/Neglected Guide: The Role of Wesley in American Methodist Theology," *Methodist History* 37:2 (1999), 75.

arose to preserve the traditional interpretation of Wesleyan theology. Many adherents of this movement eventually organized themselves into separate denominations, holiness churches, although others remained within the Methodist Church.[10]

Methodism everywhere continues to stand against all forms of oppression and exploitation and to promote social justice and inclusivity, including women and ethnic minority rights, economic fairness, and child protection rights. "Spreading scriptural holiness across these lands" implies both the personal and social dimensions because loving God with all the heart, mind, and soul implies loving one's neighbor as oneself.

One of the distinctive features of the Wesleyan Holiness tradition was John Wesley's idea of the instant moment of entire sanctification connected with Fletcher's idea of being filled with the Spirit. This core doctrine has in recent years been undergoing theological review within the Wesleyan Holiness tradition. The Methodist Church has always retained a focus on John Wesley's central doctrines, including the idea of Christian perfection, although with a respect for pluralism.

> Methodism continues to stand against all forms of oppression and exploitation and to promote social justice and inclusivity.

As noted in its *Book of Discipline* on "Sanctification and Perfection," The United Methodist Church promotes "The Distinctive Wesleyan Emphases" and affirms: "We hold that the wonder of God's acceptance and pardon does not end God's saving work, which continues to nurture our growth in grace. Through the power of the Holy Spirit, we are enabled to increase in the knowledge and love of God and in love for our neighbor. New birth is the first step in this process of sanctification. Sanctifying grace draws us toward the gift of Christian perfection, which

---

10   Cf. Melville Dieter, *The Holiness Revival of the Nineteenth Century*. Metuchen, New Jersey: The Scarecrow Press, Inc., 1980.

Wesley described as a heart 'habitually filled with the love of God and neighbor' and as 'having the mind of Christ and walking as he walked'."

Recent Methodist Scholarship and Relationships

One of the truly remarkable developments in re-emphasizing the relevance of Wesleyan theology and bringing it to the forefront of United Methodism was the scholarship of Albert C. Outler. The significance of John Wesley as a church reformer and theologian had been reawakened in 1935 with the landmark study of G. C. Cell, *The Rediscovery of John Wesley*, followed by another influential book by Bishop William R. Cannon, *The Theology of John Wesley* (1946). In the 1960s, largely through the influence and inspiration of Outler, a generation of Wesley scholars emerged and continue to produce a plethora of writings unprecedented in the history of Methodism. Among these are a new critical edition of *The Works of John Wesley*, begun as *The Oxford Edition of the Works of John Wesley* (Clarendon Press, 1975-1983) and continued as *The Bicentennial Edition of the Works of John Wesley* (Abingdon Press, 1984-).

The United Methodist Church reflects a great deal of diversity among its twelve million members, forty three thousand local churches, and thirteen seminaries, but the common core is its heritage in the Wesleyan tradition. The Pan-Methodist Commission is a body of which the United Methodist Church is one of six member churches. As a staff member officer of the Office of Christian Unity and Interreligious Relationships, Dr. Glen Alton Messer, II favorably remarked about this chapter: "I read with pleasure your essay on Christian perfection. My own doctoral research touched on the contextualization of the doctrine of Christian perfection in New England during the period ca. 1789-1845. One of the star characters of the New England region was Rev. Timothy Merritt (1775-1845) who drew heavily on John Fletcher and influenced Phoebe Palmer."

Dr. Messer also observes that "our office has been working to strengthen the UMC's relationship with the Wesleyan Holiness Connection in recent years and hopes to do much more in this regard in the near future. Certainly we all share in the Wesleyan/Methodist traditions and have a common heritage to strengthen it through the Wesleyan Holiness Connection."

The focus on Christian perfection has now become a large ecumenical umbrella for ongoing conversations among Wesleyans in many different denominations through the Wesleyan Holiness Connection. The goal is to provide the church at large with a greater understanding of what it means to love God with all one's heart, mind, and soul. One of the representatives sent by the United Methodist Church to the WHC has been Dr. Bentley L. Hartley, Associate Professor of Christian Mission and the Director of United Methodist Studies at Palmer Theological Seminary. The mutually-sensed need for ecumenical cooperation among Wesleyans/Methodists to promote its heritage is one of the central goals of the WHC.

CHAPTER 18

THE WESLEYAN CHURCH

by Robert Black and Jo Anne Lyon

*"One - That the World May Believe" was the banner over the
1968 merger which created The Wesleyan Church. Though
comparatively young, its roots are among the deepest of any
holiness denomination.*

A Rich Heritage

In the 1830s ministers and laypersons in the Methodist Episcopal
Church who became advocates for abolitionism were pressured by their
bishops to keep silent on the issue and penalized severely when they
did not. As a result, a core of the most deeply committed withdrew
from the M. E. Church and launched a new denomination in 1843,
numbering 20,000 by their second year. Emphasizing their ties to John
Wesley, whose anti-slavery views had also met with opposition a century earlier, they called their new denomination the Wesleyan Methodist
Connection of America and they pointedly named their periodical
"The True Wesleyan."

Orange Scott, who had been stripped of his office as a presiding
elder (district superintendent) in the Methodist Church, was the acknowledged leader of the new denomination. Among the other founders was Luther Lee, a notable orator, debater, and author. The Wesleyan
Methodists soon established a presence on the Underground Railroad

and extended their ministry to slaves northward into Canada and well below the Mason-Dixon Line in the South.

Along with their support for slaves, Wesleyan Methodists also championed the rights of women. The first women's rights convention in American history was held in the Wesleyan Chapel in Seneca Falls, New York, which is now a National Historic Site. In addition, Luther Lee preached the ordination sermon for Antoinette Brown, a Congregationalist who was the first woman to be ordained to the Christian ministry in the modern era. The second was a Wesleyan, Mary A. Will, in 1861.

Believing the laity to be another marginalized group, Wesleyan Methodists wrote into their first Discipline the principle of equal lay and clergy representation both in annual conferences and in their quadrennial general conferences. All of these initiatives were viewed as expressions of holiness in action.

> Echoing John Wesley, the Wesleyan *Discipline* identifies the mission of the church as "the spreading of scriptural holiness throughout every land."

After emancipation brought an end to slavery in America, many Wesleyan Methodists considered their work accomplished and returned to Methodism, joining either the Methodist Episcopal Church or the Methodist Protestants. Despite significant losses in this "Union Movement," a large majority remained with the denomination, convinced that their reason for existence was not limited to the anti-slavery cause. The impetus for reform was weakened, but in its place another expression of Wesley's "perfect love" emerged. In the fires of the Holiness Revival, holiness evangelism became the top priority.

The Holiness Revival also gave rise to the group with which the Wesleyan Methodists would one day merge. In 1897 Seth Rees and Martin Wells Knapp met in Cincinnati, Ohio to organize the Holiness Union, a non-denominational affiliation of holiness-minded believers. Rees, a powerful preacher and gifted evangelist, was the more prominent public figure of the two, while Knapp displayed remarkable talents for entrepreneurial ventures in missions, education, revivalism, publications, and compassionate ministries on behalf of the Union. Their holiness coalition soon began to act like a denomination in many ways, even ordaining Charles and Lettie Cowman on the eve of their departure for the Far East in a step of faith which eventually would give rise to the Oriental Missionary Society (OMS). In 1913, the Holiness Union became the International Apostolic Holiness Church.

Taking a page from the rapid expansion of the Church of the Nazarene, the young denomination grew through a series of mergers between 1919-1925. In the most significant of those mergers, Seth Rees, who had left his leadership role in the Holiness Union years earlier and was pastoring an independent congregation in California, led his new Pilgrim Church to unite with his former ecclesiastical body and provide for it the name it would carry to its future merger with the Wesleyan Methodists, the Pilgrim Holiness Church.

Today's Church

That merger in 1968 does not rank among the largest in Protestant history, but it has proven to be among the most successful. At merger, the aggregate membership of the new denomination was 122,000. In 2015, an average of 523,596 Wesleyans gathered for worship each week around the globe. Of that number, 234,476 were in churches in North America. The remainder represented the international reach of The Wesleyan Church in 100 countries.

In the United States and Canada, the engine of growth has been mainly large churches. At merger, only two congregations numbered more than 500 in average attendance; in 2015, that number was sixty-four. Thirty of those average more than 1,000.

Significant growth has occurred overseas as well. Since merger, the progressive policy of Global Partners, the missionary arm of the church, has aimed at making each field self-reliant. As a result, The Wesleyan Church worldwide now includes three general conferences, independent in most respects but tied together by common allegiance to what is termed the Essentials – the Wesleyan name, doctrines, agreed-upon standards of conduct, and the framework of international organization. In addition to the present North American, Philippine, and Caribbean general conferences, other regional or national bodies are moving toward the same status.

Wesleyan polity is representative, a variation on the Presbyterian model. Authority is shared among the local, district, and general levels of the church. Those levels of governance operate in a parallel structure, each with its conferences, boards, and designated leaders.

Originally denominational leadership resided in multiple general superintendents. In a momentous change in 2012, the church elected a single general superintendent for the North American General Conference. Significantly, that general superintendent was a woman, Jo Anne Lyon, formerly head of World Hope International, a relief and development organization which partners with the denomination.

The Wesleyan Church operates four liberal arts institutions in the United States (Houghton College, Indiana Wesleyan University, Oklahoma Wesleyan University, and Southern Wesleyan University), a Bible college in Canada (Kingswood University), and a seminary (Wesley Seminary on the campus of Indiana Wesleyan University). Eight other seminaries in the Wesleyan-Holiness tradition are also listed as "approved" for Wesleyan students in the U.S. and Canada. In addition, a network of Bible colleges and seminaries in other countries serves the international church.

Holiness unto the Lord

Echoing John Wesley, the Wesleyan *Discipline* identifies the mission of the church as "the spreading of scriptural holiness throughout every land." In its first general conference (1844), the Wesleyan

Methodist Connection adopted an article of religion on entire sanctification, becoming the first religious body in history to do so in that form.

Through the years The Wesleyan Church has maintained close ties to other holiness groups through coalitions like the present Wesleyan Holiness Connection. The spirit of this cooperative engagement reaches back to regional associations of the nineteenth-century holiness camp meeting movement in which Wesleyan Methodists and Pilgrims were active participants. That engagement contin-

> Along with their support for slaves, Wesleyan Methodists have championed the rights of women and the laity.

ued as the associations transitioned into the National (later, Christian) Holiness Association. Additionally, as Neo-Evangelicals began to coalesce in the 1940s, Houghton College president Stephen Paine became one of the founders of the National Association of Evangelicals, representing the holiness voice in that arena. Currently, three Wesleyans sit on the Executive Committee of NAE.

Wesleyans were also present at the creation of many cooperative ventures of holiness bodies. The first president of the Wesleyan Theological Society, Leo Cox, and the first editor of its *Wesleyan Theological Journal*, Charles Carter, were both Wesleyan Methodists. When holiness clergy women gathered for the first "Come to the Water" conference, the inaugural keynote speaker was Jo Anne Lyon.

In these and other joint endeavors, The Wesleyan Church continues to value the spirit of John Wesley: "If your heart is as my heart, give me your hand." That statement applies especially to those who share a tradition of "heart holiness."

The Article of Religion on Sanctification

According to the 2012 edition of *The Discipline of The Wesleyan Church*, ¶236:

We believe that sanctification is that work of the Holy Spirit by which the child of God is separated from sin unto God and is enabled to love God with all the heart and to walk in all His holy commandments blameless. Sanctification is initiated at the moment of justification and regeneration. From that moment there is a gradual or progressive sanctification as the believer walks with God and daily grows in grace and in a more perfect obedience to God. This prepares for the crisis of entire sanctification which is wrought instantaneously when believers present themselves as living sacrifices, holy and acceptable to God, through faith in Jesus Christ, being effected by the baptism with the Holy Spirit who cleanses the heart from all inbred sin. The crisis of entire sanctification perfects the believer in love and empowers that person for effective service. It is followed by lifelong growth in grace and the knowledge of our Lord and Savior, Jesus Christ. The life of holiness continues through faith in the sanctifying blood of Christ and evidences itself by loving obedience to God's revealed will.

SELECT BIBLIOGRAPHY

Black, Robert and Keith Drury. *The Story of The Wesleyan Church*. Indianapolis: Wesleyan Publishing House, 2012.

McLeister, Ira Ford and Roy S. Nicholson. *Conscience and Commitment: The History of the Wesleyan Methodist Church of America*. Marion, IN: Wesley Press, 1976.

Thomas, Paul Westphal and Paul William Thomas. *The Days of Our Pilgrimage: The History of the Pilgrim Holiness Church*. Marion, IN: Wesley Press, 1976.

THE STORY OF THE WESLEYAN HOLINESS CONNECTION

The Wesleyan Holiness Connection has had only one decade of life to date, but how dramatic these years have been! The growth and influence has been nothing short of amazing. Not wanting to be just another religious organization, the WHC was birthed as a relational network of churches and leaders committed to holiness in the twenty-first century. It is "a catalyst for spawning fresh ministries and relationships globally" (see O'Brien, p.143).

To enrich today's Holiness stream in the holy river of God, the WHC has created Aldersgate Press to resource a new generation of instructed and inspired leaders. It has inspired new networks and leaders in the United States and globally. It has gathered the presidents and other leaders of colleges and universities in the Wesleyan-Holiness tradition. It has linked with a range of associated ministries to enrich a common enterprise. Six of these ministries are detailed in this section, with the voices of their leaders heard clearly.

The story of one of these ministry partners, America's Christian Credit Union, is told by Mendell L. Thompson and Fawn Imboden. They highlight a Bible verse that represents well that great ministry and that of the Wesleyan Holiness Connection as a whole . . . .

> See, I (God) am doing a new thing! Now it springs up . . .
> I am making a way in the wilderness and streams in the
> wasteland. (Isaiah 43:19)

CHAPTER 19

THE WESLEYAN HOLINESS CONNECTION

by Christopher D. O'Brien

When asked how the Wesleyan Holiness "Consortium"[1] started and developed, principal founder Kevin Mannoia often responds: "There was no master plan. There was no grand strategy." The idea and formation grew over a long period of time through conversations, meetings, and a study group. The purpose of this chapter is to offer a brief account of the beginning, development, and functions of what has become known as the Wesleyan Holiness Connection.

Guiding Influences

Although the story of the Wesleyan Holiness Connection began with three friends having a breakfast conversation in 2002, it had its nascent beginnings in Kevin Mannoia's childhood when his family served as Free Methodist missionaries in Brazil. Growing up there, Mannoia encountered a diversity of streams of Christianity that embodied the gospel of Christ in unique ways. For him, these various expressions of the

---

1 In 2016, the Board of Directors and Steering Committee of the WHC changed the name to the "Wesleyan Holiness Connection" as a more relevant term while also underscoring the relational nature of the organization consistent with its Wesleyan identity.

gospel were an eye-opening experience that highlighted the constructive contribution – whether small or large – that each church tradition offers the one, holy, apostolic church as a whole in its global contexts. This experience, along with others along the way, created his desire to explore, understand, and communicate the voice of his own Wesleyan-Holiness tradition as one of the many tributaries of the larger river of God.

> Growing up in Brazil, Kevin Mannoia encountered a diversity of streams of Christianity and learned that each offers a contribution to the church as a whole.

In the years that followed his return to the United States, Mannoia had influential experiences that shaped his desire for what would become the Wesleyan Holiness Connection. First, he encountered negative views of the Wesleyan-Holiness tradition among scholars and laity. While attending a theological conference on holiness, for instance, he heard a scholar note that the Holiness movement does not have the ability "to renew itself, and its churches have become merely a repository of historical information."[2] This comment irritated Mannoia. After all, he had been part of the transformative work of the holiness message through his family's experiences abroad, as well as having witnessed its current relevancy in global contexts.

Second, Mannoia gained a better understanding of the influential nature of the Wesleyan-Holiness message in shaping the global church in his own leadership roles. He was a bishop of the Free Methodist Church and subsequently led the National Association of Evangelicals. However, he noticed that the message of holiness was now often overlooked and/or viewed as archaic and not sophisticated enough for modern Christianity, even though it represented the fastest growing segments of the church in the world. Moreover, he also observed that the Wesleyan-Holiness movement had become a loosely connected

2 This quote is taken from Kevin W. Mannoia and Don Thorsen, eds., *The Holiness Manifesto* (Grand Rapids, MI: Eerdmans, 2008), 3.

group of denominations with different emphases – e.g., social justice, entire sanctification, the role of the Holy Spirit, and diverse approaches to pursuing social and individual holiness. What was lacking was a means to connect these various denominations that share the common mission of spreading scriptural holiness across the land.

Formation of the Wesleyan Holiness Connection

The Wesleyan Holiness Connection began with a breakfast meeting in late 2002 when Kevin Mannoia met with Don Dayton and David Bundy, two well-known scholars of the holiness movement. Their conversation focused on the neglect of the holiness tradition as an important voice and contributor to the global church. They decided to address this oversight by creating an academic event that would address the effects of holiness "being submerged in the history of the church."

For Mannoia, however, this study group was not merely to be an academic enterprise, but also a means of involving church leaders and serving the church in shaping its future mission in a new century. Several Wesleyan-Holiness denominational leaders agreed to support the Wesleyan Holiness Study Project with financial commitments and the annual participation of their scholars for three years. The Study Project consisted of about forty scholars who represented thirteen historically Wesleyan-Holiness denominations. The objective was to "commit to a fresh articulation of holiness in the 21st century."

In May, 2004, the inaugural meeting of the Wesleyan-Holiness Study Project convened at Azusa Pacific University and included representatives from the following holiness traditions: Church of the Nazarene, Free Methodist, Brethren in Christ, Salvation Army, Evangelical Friends, Christian and Missionary Alliance, and the Church of God (Anderson). Additionally, America's Christian Credit Union made a commitment to the Study Project because its mission was consistent with the Credit Union's future path of service.

The theme for the meeting was global and historical views on holiness. The papers presented addressed and highlighted a variety of issues and topics related to holiness in its past and current forms. Based on the presentations and the discussions that followed, this study group created a three-year agenda by identifying writing assignments, intended outcomes, and potential next steps. This work continued for four years and experienced an ebb and flow of growth in participants.

Eventually several more denominations joined the Study Project, including: the International Church of the Foursquare Gospel, International Pentecostal Holiness Church, Shield of Faith, Church of God in Christ, and the Church of God (Cleveland). These denominations represented the broader scope of the Wesleyan-Holiness tradition that have their roots in the holiness-influenced Azusa Street revival and the subsequent split between the Pentecostal and Revivalist currents of the church. For Mannoia, the addition of these churches was a positive indication of the growing desire for unity among a tradition that has a divided history.

> The WHC is a relational network of churches committed to holiness and empowering leaders to embody relevant engagement with the world.

In its four meetings, the Wesleyan Holiness Study Project produced two significant documents, "The Holiness Manifesto" and "Fresh Eyes on Holiness: Living Out the Holiness Manifesto." These defined and continue to guide the nature and contemporary purpose of the holiness movement. Moreover, they function as helpful tools for training pastors and lay leaders. In particular, "The Holiness Manifesto" addresses what it means to be God's holy people and then offers ways for church leaders to engage their congregations in pursuit of holiness. The document "Fresh Eyes on Holiness" identifies the diverse dimensions of holiness in the life of God's community.[3]

---

3   Both documents are available at the end of this present volume.

On September 15, 2006, nearing the end of the initial commitment to the WH Study Project, Mannoia convened a one-day meeting with the denominational heads in Dallas, Texas, to consider the work completed and explore possible next steps. In four years, the Study Project had produced many papers on holiness, two manifestos, cultivated positive relationships among the denominations, and soon would publish a book on holiness with Eerdmans Press. As a result, the group decided there was a future to this nascent movement. After prayerful consideration, they decided to change the name and create an ongoing Connection of churches and leaders to expand its mission through regional networks, research and writing, and the development of leaders in the holiness stream of the church.

Consequently, the Wesleyan Holiness Connection was birthed as a relational network of churches and leaders committed to holiness in the twenty-first century. A Steering Committee and Board of Directors were created with representatives from each of the regional networks and denominations. Two years later, the Connection was incorporated in the State of California and this process crystalized its corporate identity. The Connection's vision and purpose are guided by four convictions: (1) explore what holiness looks like in the twenty-first century; (2) develop unity within and among the participating holiness churches and denominations; (3) voice the significance of the holiness tradition within the broader church; and (4) identify and develop the importance of holiness in the future mission of the church.

The Wesleyan Holiness Connection has come to pursue its vision and purpose in at least three particular ways, with additional detail on each available elsewhere in this volume.

- **Regional Networks:** The ministry presence of the Wesleyan Holiness Connection occurs primarily in and through Regional Networks. Initially they formed across the United States. Internationally, there now are networks in Brazil, Kenya, Philippines, the United Kingdom, and

Canada. These networks are comprised of denominational leaders and pastors who meet regularly and conduct annual Pastors'/Leaders' Days. The purpose of these annual
meetings is to resource leaders by bringing them together
for fellowship, worship, and seminars on selected themes
that address holiness in the twenty-first century. (See following chapters.)

• **Associated Ministries:** A range of ministry groups bring
together leaders with a common interest to explore how
the Wesleyan-Holiness tradition has and should shape
their particular work. Currently there are five such ministries associated in various ways with the WHC, with their
individual stories told in individual chapters following.

• **Aldersgate Press:** In 2011 the Wesleyan Holiness
Connection created Aldersgate Press in order to provide
opportunity for fresh voices to publish significant materi-
al that fuels the holiness movement in today's diverse contexts. Barry L. Callen of the Church of God (Anderson)
was elected the Editor and a national Publications Team
was named to oversee publication processes and standards. See chapter 20.

Conclusion

Although there was no master plan or strategy in place for creating the
Wesleyan Holiness Connection, it became a reality through the gradual
process of conversations, commitments, and research. What started as
a study project to explore the nature and significance of holiness in the
twenty-first century has now become so much more, including being
a catalyst for spawning fresh ministries and relationships globally. The
Connection continues to serve this mission by following the nudges of

the Holy Spirit, empowering pastors and leaders to more authentically embody their denominational heritages, and boldly leading in relevant engagement with the world as God's holy people.

CHAPTER 20

ALDERSGATE PRESS

by Barry L. Callen, Editor

T he initial publishing effort of the Wesleyan Holiness Connection was the release in 2006 of the *Holiness Manifesto*. It grew out of the concerns and consensus of participants in the Wesleyan Holiness Study Project convened on the campus of Azusa Pacific University in California. This was followed in 2008 by a multi-authored book of the same title edited by Kevin Mannoia and Don Thorsen and published by Wm. B. Eerdmans Publishing Co.

While an excellent beginning for getting the vision and work of the Wesleyan Holiness Connection more widely known, these publications were considered to be only a beginning. Many more resources were needed as catalysts for the renewal of today's churches through the dynamic of Christian holiness.

Birth of Aldersgate Press

The Wesleyan Holiness Study Project began in 2004 and soon matured into the Wesleyan Holiness Connection. The Study Project produced two significant essay documents that sought to freshly articulate the vision of unity and power resident in the Christian holiness message. These documents, soon widely distributed through multiple channels, helped launch the publishing history of the WHC.

The first of these documents, released in February, 2006, was the *Holiness Manifesto*. Then in March, 2007, came *Fresh Eyes on Holiness: Living Out the Holiness Manifesto* (the full texts of both are available in this volume). The major volume *The Holiness Manifesto* (Wm. B. Eerdmans Publishing Co., 2008) soon followed, drawing together writers from many Christian traditions. These comprised a great beginning, but only the beginning.

Aldersgate Press, arm of the WHC, publishes resources for the renewal of today's churches through the dynamic of Christian holiness.

It soon became obvious that the WHC's vision of a publishing ministry was too extensive to be accomplished by an occasional release through an established publisher not involved with the Connection. Accordingly, Aldersgate Press was formed in 2011 as the publications arm of the WHC. "Aldersgate," of course, is that street in London, England, where a critical event in the spiritual life of John Wesley helped launch a holiness revival in the eighteenth century. The prayer in 2011 was that a new Aldersgate Press would be an instrument used of God for a similar purpose in the twenty-first century.

The new Press represented the coordinated effort of the many church bodies that form the WHC. Their joint intention was to fuel with fresh writing the growing interest in and influence of Christian holiness among church leaders in the twenty-first century. The organization of this effort was to be as simple as possible, avoiding the costly duplication of staffing and expertise available elsewhere.

Five people with differing gifts and denominational affiliations were named as the Publications Team to govern Press policies and operations under the supervision of the WHC Board of Directors. Elected as the founding Editor was Barry L. Callen, one of the writers of the *Holiness Manifesto*, the WHC denominational representative from the Church of God (Anderson), author of several earlier volumes on the subject of Christian holiness, and longtime Editor of the *Wesleyan Theological Journal*. The Publisher initially would be the president and founder of the WHC, Kevin Mannoia. By 2016 his duties were so heavy that the role of Aldersgate's publisher was shifted to Dr. Jon Kulaga, Provost of Asbury University in Kentucky.

While leaders, churches, and affiliated educational institutions and other affiliated ministries comprising the WHC would be the primary focus market and distribution network for Aldersgate, others soon would be included in order to provide a wider reach into all segments of the church in North America and even globally.

The Vision and Mission of the Press

The originating publishing vision centered in the need to construct a pipeline connecting experienced and new authors who would creatively write about the biblical revelation of God's holiness and holy living in our day. Such writing would further fuel the movement of church leaders who are seeking a fresh, practical, and relevant unifying message to focus their mission for Christ today. The following was Aldersgate's formal mission statement:

> The mission of Aldersgate Press is to be a communication channel extending the ministry of the Wesleyan Holiness Connection. Of particular concern is the encouraging of a new generation of authors to focus on the growing interest in transformed Christian living by appropriating in their writings the meanings and implications of Christian holiness for contemporary believers, cultures, and structures. Such timely and creative focus will be a motivating force to invigorate particularly those in the traditional holiness and pentecostal movements toward greater power, passion, and unity in contemporary church mission.

How would such a mission be accomplished? Resources were very limited. Therefore, editing, printing, and distribution activities of Aldersgate were designed to be operated as efficiently as possible, relying as possible on volunteer assistance. A partnership was established with an existing publisher. Initially this partner was Emeth Press, Lexington, Kentucky, headed by Laurence Wood of Asbury Theological Seminary. After the initial years of operation, the partnership shifted to Lamp Post Publishers, Spring Valley, California, headed by Brett Burner.

To ensure the professional competence of submitted materials, as well as their practical relevance to life in the churches today, a detailed process of manuscript review was established. It includes a team of reviewers outside the Press staff, individuals skilled in the subject at hand and able to judge the likely reception and impact of the proposed publication. Such judgments are received prior to each publication decision of the Publications Team that is comprised of the Publisher, Editor, printing partner, and two others – Donald Thorsen, a seasoned Wesleyan scholar, and Marlene Chase, an experienced editor and writer in the Salvation Army tradition.

> The Press highlights the meanings and implications of Christian holiness, invigorating believers toward greater power, passion, and unity.

Aldersgate's Publishing History

The intent always has been to work from a strong biblical base in the production of materials that are (1) readily accessible to a modern readership and (2) have practical relevance to actually living out the call to holiness in contemporary settings. Thus, of concern have been holiness-related issues like linking daily work and weekly worship, finding a new vocabulary for holiness, assuring that marketing and evangelism are done with honor, exploring how holiness should function in all aspects of the life of a university campus, and learning how to die with holy dignity. Early Aldersgate titles have been:

1. *Maximum Faith* by George Barna (2011). From a Christian perspective, the purpose of life's journey is to become the person God conceived you to be. That maturation requires you to undergo transforming experiences. But how does the journey progress? What options do you have en route to the final destination?

2. *Masterful Living: New Vocabulary for the Holy Life* by Kevin Mannoia (2012). Much of the language used about Christian holiness has become stilted, stereotyped, outdated. Here is a new vocabulary for the holy life in our new time.

3. *Heart & Life: Rediscovering Holy Living* edited by Barry L. Callen and Don Thorsen (2012). Christian holiness is personal and experiential, but also open to serious scholarly probing. Here are presentations by recognized Wesleyan scholars exploring the breadth and depth of the teaching and past practice of Christian holiness.

4. *Work that Matters: Bridging the Divide between Work and Worship* by Kevin Brown and Michael Wiese (2013). Christian holiness definitely should impact how we live our lives in our workplaces. Too many of us build a wall between our work through the week and our worship on Sunday.

5. *A Good Walk Home: A Parable of Living and Dying Well* by Larry Walkemeyer (2013). Christian holiness is for more than living as God wishes. It also is for dying in a way that God enables. This is a simple and yet profound journey from life to death and on into greater

life for the dying and those care givers who stand by and serve.

6. *Color Me Holy: Holy God . . . Holy People* by Hubert P. Harriman and Barry L. Callen (2013). Holiness is God's nature and desire for all true disciples. "Be ye holy, for I am holy" says the Lord. This book is available in English, Spanish, and Swahili.

7. *Catch Your Breath! Exhaling Death & Inhaling Life* by Barry L. Callen (2014). Here is a fresh metaphor for expressing Christian holiness, one with balance between the holy life offered by God's grace and the intentional disciplines required of the believer, the private spiritual experiences and the social demands of living them out.

8. *Higher Higher Education: Integrating Holiness into All of Campus Life* by Jonathan S. Raymond (2015). The formation of a faith perspective on all of life and the shaping of student character are goals that should permeate all aspects of the life of a Christian campus.

9. *Biblical Heights for Today's Valleys: Mountain-top Revelations of Christian Holiness* by H. Ray Dunning (2015). Christian holiness has a solid biblical base. Its several dimensions of insight and implication were revealed by God on a range of mountaintops. Dunning guides the reader to these great locations and reviews what is learned at each place.

10. *Honorable Influence* by David Hagenbuch, with a Foreword by Peter Greer. This is a Christian guide to

marketing. In a world dominated by sellers, advertisers, and consumers, including the church (evangelism), here is a great tool for determining how followers of Jesus can be influencers and do it honorably.

11. *The Holy River of God* edited by Barry L. Callen and written by many authors representing the numerous church bodies and affiliated ministries networked with the Wesleyan Holiness Connection. This is a history of the nature and mission of the WHC, including its nature, mission, constituents, and accomplishments. Included are (1) broad historical perspectives on the history of the Holiness stream of Christianity globally and (2) key resource documents from the WHC on important social issues of today.

Additional Partnerships

The publishing partners in the United States have been Emeth Press, Lexington, Kentucky, and Lamp Post Publishers, Spring Valley, California. These, however, have been supplemented by others. Central have been World Gospel Mission, Marion, Indiana, and especially its related African Gospel Church in Kenya, East Africa. The Aldersgate book *Color Me Holy* was republished by this African church in further partnership with Publish-4-All, a global print-on-demand network. Another Christian ministry affiliated with the Wesleyan Holiness Connection, America's Christian Credit Union, Glendora, California, has been especially generous and encouraging in multiple ways.

WHC NETWORKS

CHAPTER 21

REGIONAL NETWORKS: UNITED STATES

by Carla and Charles Sunberg

The mighty rivers of earth have powerful currents which are being harnessed to provide energy to much of the world. In the same way the Wesleyan/Holiness streams and tributaries are uniting into a mighty river of witness to the transformational power of God's Holy Spirit. One of the ways in which this has become manifest is through a series of regional networks which have developed across the United States.

The Early Vision

The vision of pastors and other leaders gathering for connecting, mutual support and encouragement came early in the development of the Wesleyan Holiness Connection. A tendency among Wesleyan/Holiness churches has been to work in isolation, often unaware of sister denominations and leaders, even within one's own community. The Wesleyan/Holiness voice has often suffered from a lack of inertia because leaders have remained pooled within their own small tributaries.

The Southern California Holiness Pastor's day in 2010 began a movement which simply could not be stopped. The regional leaders had prayed that God would meet with the group and inspire the pastors with a deeper understanding of our unity in holiness. They prayed that holiness as their common mission would become a priority as the denominations networked together. The different regional directors addressed the variety of perspectives on holy living. Those presenting included:

> David Winn – Church of God
> Kimberly Dirmann – Foursquare
> Jerry Ferguson – Nazarene
> Steve Fitch – Free Methodist
> Perry Engle – Brethren in Christ
> Steven Bradley – Salvation Army

Suddenly it was discovered that each tributary had something to offer to the greater stream and the result was a more profound message of holiness.

From across the varying denominations there arose an awareness of others with a similar passion and the resultant power to be found in unity. The tributaries began to flow together to become a mighty stream that would give rise to regional networks in California, Washington, Oregon, Indiana, Ohio, Missouri, Pennsylvania, Florida, and beyond. The WHC has provided leadership to nurture and coordinate these diverse efforts.

Models

The character of each regional network of the Wesleyan Holiness Connection has varied according to area leadership and felt needs, reflecting the unique contexts of ministry in which the Wesleyan/ Holiness churches are found. Kevin Mannoia has been the catalyst to bring together regional leaders who have expressed an interest in creating a network.

Initial gatherings have brought together bishops, district superintendents, area leaders and territorial commanders to consider opportunities and benefits of partnership. This unity and commitment among leadership is absolutely vital to the success of the regional network phenomenon. These leaders at times have met before launching a regional network, taking the time to develop relationships and mutual direction.

Most networks have developed into a gathering, such as an annual "Holiness Pastors and Leaders Day." The expansion beyond pastors has been intentional as God continues to raise up leaders who are passionate about the message of holiness. The "Day" is often hosted on the campus of a university or a large local church. The Wesleyan Holiness Connection has been grateful for the support of local institutions who have graciously opened their doors to these gatherings.

A tendency among Wesleyan/Holiness churches has been to work in isolation, often unaware of sister denominations and leaders, even within one's own community.

Meeting following breakfast and remaining until mid-afternoon, round-table settings have created an atmosphere for learning and networking. Plenary sessions mixed with prayer, lunch, and workshops have resulted in a clearer understanding of the message of holiness as well as unity and partnership among the represented denominations. Question and answer periods have been positively received as these days have provided an open environment for serious conversation. In some cases, regional leaders have begun meeting together in a retreat setting for a days-long time of prayer and renewal.

Several regional networks have embraced the opportunity to resource those present. At times there have been exhibitors with books, informational and other materials to enhance ministry. Helping to support those who promote the Wesleyan/Holiness message beyond denominational lines helps to strengthen the stream. Aldersgate Press, the publishing arm of the Wesleyan Holiness Connection continually produces new resources to strengthen the message of holiness.

Guest Speakers

Through the years a number of voices have added to the Wesleyan/Holiness conversation by serving as plenary speakers. Crossing a myriad of denominational and church lines, unity has been found in diversity. Speakers have numbered more than twenty-five outstanding voices from a wide range of denominations and para-church organizations.

In addition to these plenary speakers, local denominational leaders often have filled the role of workshop presenters. Practical aspects of local church ministry, social engagement and personal spiritual formation have been important in these Wesleyan/Holiness conversations.

Testimonials

For some currently engaged in Christian ministry, the message of holiness has not been articulated for the modern missional context. Younger leaders have responded very positively to the establishment of a new vocabulary that provides for fresh expressions of holiness. The positive message of transformation experienced in holiness is one which resonates widely.

Regional Network gatherings have brought together bishops, district superintendents, area leaders and territorial commanders to consider the opportunities and benefits of partnership.

When holiness is lived out through effective mission, it engages with society and contemporary needs. Speaking on issues across a broad spectrum, from human trafficking to pornography to the marginalized of society, the holiness message and challenge is one which is being embraced by our younger leadership. The question-and-answer sessions have proved especially fruitful as we wrestle with both language and engagement from a holiness perspective.

Over and over, pastors and other leaders have expressed their gratitude for these regional networks that have brought together like-minded individuals who are passionate about ministry. Not only do those in attendance leave refreshed and armed with tools for proclaiming the holiness message, but partnerships and friendships develop that become transformational. If our varied denominations work in a vacuum, pastors can potentially be left lonely and discouraged. Realizing that there is a partner within the local community, someone with similar passions, has become empowering.

Women are appreciative of the holiness days of these Networks because they provide a platform and voice for female clergy. Simply looking across the room and realizing that there are many women called to vocational ministry is encouraging, especially when women are featured as speakers. This is a welcome reminder that God-called women have always had a significant place within the history of the holiness movement.

While each Network gathering has its own local flavor, the resources commonly showcased have proved invaluable. Whether from the WHC's own Aldersgate Press or from other sources, published resources are made available at the regional events. As we share our writings with one another we provide greater depth and strength to the holiness message.

We Are Better Together

For far too long we have driven past the churches of our sister denominations and failed to stop to get to know one another. These WHC Regional Networks have created that space where we stop, fellowship around the table, eat a meal together, and learn that we have partners in ministry right in our own neighborhoods.

The relationships that have developed are creating a bond which will unite us together in preaching the holiness message and practicing a lifestyle of holiness that engages with our communities. These beautiful reflections of the uniting and sending activities of Christ, when magnified among our holiness churches through networking, can make an eternal difference. We are better together!

CHAPTER 22

THE WESLEYAN HOLINESS CONNECTION
IN BRAZIL AND GLOBALLY

by Ildo Mello and Clovis Paradela

The Wesleyan Holiness Connection (WHC) in Brazil provides a wonderful forum for sharing ideas and enjoying fellowship among churches of Wesleyan origin that are finding increased unity in their work together. The Brazilian WHC emerged through several interacting forces that converged in the formation of the Conexao Wesleyana de Santidade (WHC) in Brazil.

Beginnings of Conexao Wesleyana de Santidade (WHC Brazil)

Early in the new century, Bishop Adriel Maia of the Methodist Church in São Paulo met with other denominational leaders motivated by concern over the distance between churches with a common Wesleyan origin. Not long after, in 2008, came the formation of an initiative in which pastors of similar heritage met regularly to shepherd each other. These gatherings continue and were a vital precursor to the establishment of the WHC in Brazil. This initiative brought together bishops, superintendents, and key leaders of the Methodist,

Free Methodist, Wesleyan Methodist, Salvation Army, and Nazarene churches.

Meanwhile in Rio de Janeiro, Clóvis Paradela, a key Methodist leader, formed a group through social media for dialogue and mutual support. It included many bishops, superintendents, pastors, and other leaders of the specific churches with Wesleyan origins. In these dialogues it became clear that these churches were much more alike than thought. Even their shortcomings were similar.

With the support of Methodist Bishop Paulo Lockman, Clóvis along with Antônio Faleiro Sobrinho went to the Orthodox Methodist Church to open a dialogue with Bishop José Francisco and a few pastors, as well as Robson Nascimento who was appointed by Bishop José Ildo to represent the Free Methodist Church in Rio de Janeiro. Bishop Onaldo Rodrigues Pereira of the Wesleyan Methodist Church of the state of Rio de Janeiro and Lázaro Aguiar Valvassoura, at the time president of the Church of the Nazarene in Brazil, also received the dialogue proposal with enthusiasm.

> The WHC in Brazil provides a forum for sharing ideas and fellowship among churches of Wesleyan origin.

In 2010, Kevin Mannoia spoke with Ildo Mello about the growth of the Wesleyan Holiness Connection in the United States, and requested that he convene leaders in São Paulo during a visit he would be making. Ildo made contact with Clóvis in Rio and when it became evident that more leaders from Rio wanted to travel to São Paulo to attend the meeting, Clovis requested that Mannoia alter plans and have a meeting in both São Paulo and Rio. These two gatherings occurred during the month of July, 2010, first in the Cascadura Methodist Church of Rio de Janeiro and a few days later at the Free Methodist Seminary in São Paulo with the special participation of Mannoia in both.

During the meeting in Rio there was experienced powerful moments during the messages brought by Mannoia, Lockman, and other key national leaders including José Francisco da Silva (Orthodox

Methodist), Edgard Chagas (Salvation Army), Elisiário Alves dos Santos (Wesleyan Methodist), Pedro Paulo Matos (Nazarene), and Ildo Mello (Free Methodist). Although originally expecting a group of 20-30, the enthusiasm of the leaders drew approximately 400 pastors during the afternoon and evening sessions of that memorable day.

Development of Strong Relational Bonds

Clovis Paradela, serving as President of Bennett University Center in Rio and deeply involved in the Methodist region, served as Regional Coordinator for the Connection in Rio. In São Paulo, Ildo Mello was encouraged into the Regional Coordinator role and served as a national point of contact for the WHC. These coordinators were instrumental in forming the Connection in other cities as well. Misael Lemos, at that time the Methodist Superintendent in the national capital of Brasilia, initiated the Connection in Brasilia with a series of visits by Mannoia in early 2011 after the Connection was formed in Rio and São Paulo.

For the first time ever, the WHC brought together in dialogue and collaborative effort the leaders and pastors of the many growing churches in Brazil: Methodist, Free Methodist, Wesleyan Methodist, Church of the Nazarene, Salvation Army, Holiness, Grace Community, Renewed Methodist, International Methodist, and Alliance Methodist. These leaders began to meet regularly, developing strong relational bonds and creating a community in which they learned from one another the story of each denomination as a way of understanding more completely holiness in the Wesleyan tradition. These meetings in the three original Regional Networks focused on:

- learning from one another
- providing training for pastors and leaders
- discussing issues related to holiness in the 21st century
- prayer together
- planning events in order to promote holiness.

The energy and reputation of these gatherings quickly spread among all the denominations throughout Brazil. Soon requests from leaders across the country prompted Ildo and Clovis to catalyze meetings in other cities, which has led to the formation of Regional Networks of the Conexao Wesleyana de Santidade in other major urban centers of Brazil:

1. Belo Horizonte – MG
2. Brasília – DF
3. Fortaleza – CE
4. Joinvile – SC
5. Rio de Janeiro – RJ – Rio e Baixada Fluminense
6. São Paulo – SP
7. Sul Fluminense – RJ
8. Região dos Lagos Fluminense – RJ

Riding the wave of enthusiasm over newly found unity and fellowship centered on holiness in the Wesleyan tradition, one of the notable early events involved a celebration of John Wesley's heartwarming experience. Ten months after the initial meetings in São Paulo and Rio, the WHC leaders in São Paulo held a major rally in the Ibirapuera city stadium to which over 8,000 people came. All of the national church leaders were present, demonstrating a newly forged unity in mission to their people. The message was clear that holiness as a unifying message was marking a new chapter in the history of the Christian community in Brazil.

A unique feature of the Brazilian networks involves much fellowship enabled through social media by means of Whatsapp, Facebook, and Google groups. At the first meeting with Mannoia and seventeen leaders in São Paulo, the group took the name *Fraternidade Wesleyana de Santidade*. This original name was used until a group was started in Joinvile, Santa Catarina, in January of 2016. They referred to their first gathering as a "Connection."

During his annual visit to the WHC networks in Brazil, Mannoia noted the new name reference and discussed with Ildo Mello and Clovis Paradela the possibility of adopting it more broadly. Their encouragement and support prompted Mannoia to present the idea to the WHC Board of Directors in the United States, which subsequently supported the change of name (dropping the word "Consortium"), thereby deepening the reflection of the Wesleyan heritage as truly a "connection."

At a time when much division exists and new churches of diverse doctrines and structures are proliferating, we see the growing Conexao Wesleyana de Santidade as a great testimony to the world of unity in the Body of Christ rallied around the message of holiness.

Additional WHC Initiatives Globally

Based on the principle that the Wesleyan Holiness Connection does not go into a location unless there is clearly expressed interest and desire on the part of local church leaders, the WHC trusts the Holy Spirit to open any new doors of expansion. Thus, the WHC always is acting in response to the nudge of the Spirit. Such a nudge has come from various places in the world beyond Brazil.

Kenya

Upon discovering the existence of the WHC, the bishop of the African Gospel Church in Kenya, Robert Langat, reached out through the then president of World Gospel Mission, Hubert Harriman. Harriman had just concluded writing the book *Color Me Holy* with Barry Callen for Aldersgate Press of the WHC, which book subsequently was reprinted in Nairobi and distributed to the pastors of the church in Kenya.

After corresponding and coordinating with various other denominational leaders in Kenya, Kevin Mannoia met in Nairobi with approximately forty leaders of Kenyan denominations for a half-day meeting to discuss the relevance of holiness in the Kenyan context.

Strong interest ensued in creating an ongoing relationship among the leaders. Since then, the Harriman/Callen book has been translated into a local language and distributed widely for the education and inspiration of pastors.

Philippines

At the catalytic prompting of the Wesleyan Holiness Connection's Freedom Network, national church leaders in the Philippines were contacted about the idea of meeting to discuss the growing scourge of human trafficking in the Philippine context. Representatives of the Freedom Network had developed regular contact and interest with a few of these leaders.

> The WHC, going where interest is expressed by local church leaders, has found such interest around the world.

The WHC was seen as a viable and helpful means of gathering the national leaders regarding a common interest in the specific agenda of anti-trafficking, and a more general collaboration in the mission of articulating holiness in relevant ways for the 21st century. The first meeting of a Manila regional network was held when Kevin Mannoia convened denominational leaders at Alliance Graduate School in Manila. Melvin Aquino of the Wesleyan Church in the Philippines picked up the role of coordinator and is continuing to maintain relationships and interest in the effort.

United Kingdom

After searching for a possible convening entity for the Wesleyan Holiness movement in England, Deirdre Brower Latz, President of Nazarene Theological College in Manchester, contacted Kevin Mannoia about the possibility of a network of the Wesleyan Holiness Connection in the United Kingdom. The two worked on developing a comprehensive list of key regional leaders in the UK.

The goal, as in any other location, was to convene leaders to bring synergy and integrated focus to the Wesleyan Holiness movement as represented in the many separate groups with ministry in the UK. At the publication of this volume, a first gathering of regional leaders in Manchester is planned to explore the ongoing possibilities for unity in representing the Wesleyan Holiness stream of the church in England and Scotland.

CHAPTER 23

THE WHC PRESIDENTS' NETWORK

by James L. Edwards

A. BEGINNINGS AND GOALS

L and was granted by the Virginia Company in 1619 for America's first university. The goal was to combine classical learning and the Christian faith for the sake of cultivating "the humane person." This new school in the British colonies would provide an education worthy of directing all personal and public affairs. Unfortunately, disease and violence ended this venture in 1622. Soon, however, faith and learning joined forces again with the founding of Harvard College in 1636. This would be the first in a series of new colonial institutions designed to lift high the banner of Christ in the context of serious academic study and life preparation.

In general, collegiate education in the new world "found its parent and main sponsor in the Christian churches. Religion was unashamedly recognized as the keystone of the educational arch . . . . The God worshiped by Christians was recognized as the ground of truth and, therefore, the guiding light and ruling principle in the education of the young."[1] The numerous Christian denominations in the new United

---

1   Barry L. Callen, *Enriching Mind & Spirit* (Anderson University Press, 2007), 14.

States provided a tremendous impulse for college founding. New schools were motivated by the need for an educated ministry, strengthening denominational loyalty, and countering the "secularistic" influences soon spreading throughout the nation.

This judgment states well the present circumstance: "In conventional higher education there is little room for the education of the heart. Colleges and universities in the Wesleyan Holiness tradition are well placed to bring head, heart, and life together."[2] Toward this end of head-heart-life integration, the Wesleyan Holiness Connection created the WHC Presidents' Network, bringing together annually leaders of many of today's colleges and universities in this stream of the church.

Presidents of independent and church-related colleges and universities share a secret that comes out of their desire to connect and collaborate. They often attend conferences and join associations to be well informed for their challenging world of leadership. However, they almost universally agree that the best of such experiences will be found around the edges, in the corridors and coffee shops where leaders chat between sessions. They associate and return often because they are in the fellowship of those who understand the complicated and challenging worlds they lead. With generosity of spirit, they find an enrichment that is deeper than the reporting of current events or the latest administrative research. They find richness in sharing life with those who know, and especially those who come to their assignments out of a common faith and within the same theological stream of life.

> Collegiate education in the young United States found its main sponsor in the Christian churches, with religion the keystone of the educational arch.

Those who commit to a well-supported association of kindred spirits are finding sustaining benefits for their demanding work. They are

2   Jonathan S. Raymond, *Higher Higher Education: Integrating Holiness into All of Campus Life* (Aldersgate Press, 2015), 25.

finding the grounding needed to lead in challenging times. A program centered in the leadership of presidents is practical and reflects the value of relationships among the members rather than relying on the work of outside experts. Attending presidents value hearing from one another.

The idea of a presidential forum came out of concerns of the Wesleyan Holiness Connection. This Connection consists of bishops, overseers, superintendents, general directors, and other national pastoral leaders from a wide range of Wesleyan-Holiness bodies. Leaders who founded this association saw the value of bringing together presidents of their affiliated institutions of higher education for the same benefits that were enriching their own work.

Supporting churches look to related colleges, universities, and theological schools to develop leaders and sustain a culture of ministry and service in the rich traditions of Wesleyan-Holiness thought. They agreed to encourage presidential leaders to get together for the benefit of all. From this encouragement came the first of such gatherings. Such a simple but compelling idea was at once attractive and sustainable. This gathering expanded from a handful of presidents to more than 60 across the years.

The WHC Presidents' Network is designed to bring together annually leaders of many of today's colleges and universities in this Christian tradition in order to:

1. Further involve institutions of higher education and their leaders in the Wesleyan-Holiness mission in today's world;

2. Clarify the fundamental contribution of Wesleyan-Holiness thinking and practice in shaping the enterprise of higher education; and

3. Encourage presidents to freshly focus on their spiritual and theological heritage as a means of anchoring them in the changing culture of the twenty-first century.

It made sense to attach these gatherings to the annual meeting of the Council for Christian Colleges and Universities (CCCU), the largest presidential association for leaders of Christ-centered colleges and universities. Adding a half-day to the annual meeting of the CCCU, usually held in Washington, D.C., was economically feasible and respectful of busy presidential schedules. The Wesleyan Holiness Presidents' Network enjoys the encouragement of the leaders of the CCCU.

The agenda for these gatherings has always been practical, centered on ways to bring the Wesleyan-Holiness emphasis to campuses. Scholars from these campuses are occasionally invited to present papers and lead discussions. The witness of various leaders about their own understandings and their work has made these gatherings a top priority for a rich seminar of ideas.

These are times when all Christian colleges and universities are facing challenges almost unprecedented in scope and complexity. Being grounded in a rich theological tradition provides leaders an essential basis for effective work. The Wesleyan perspective gives a wonderful context for doing this work of Christian higher education.

We turn now to testimonials of some presidential leaders who are making a profound difference on their campuses and who are finding their way together as they share in their Wesleyan-Holiness witness.

B. PRESIDENTIAL EXPERIENCES AND REFLECTIONS

#1   Jim J. Adams, President
Life Pacific College, San Dimas, California

God opened a door more than a decade ago for Life Pacific College (LPC) and our affiliated denomination, The Foursquare Church, to become founding members of the Wesleyan Holiness Connection (WHC). We share the richness of mutual theology and faith practice, as well as common roots in the greater holiness movement foundational to LPC and the early twentieth-century evangelistic ministry of our founder, Aimee Semple McPherson. From her childhood and teen years in the holiness tradition of the Methodist Church of rural Canada during the early 1900s and her later involvement with The Salvation Army and The Assemblies of God, McPherson was well versed in holiness theology. She established an educational system within The Foursquare Church that embraces social justice, "shoe-leather gospel," practical application of the Bible to everyday living, and a global perspective of the gospel that became a cornerstone of The Foursquare Church and the contemporary expression of academics and student preparation for life and service at LPC.

> The agenda for the WHC presidents has been practical, centered on ways to increase the Wesleyan-Holiness emphasis on campuses.

Our affiliation with the WHC was birthed in relationship first between my colleague and friend Kevin Mannoia and Jack W. Hayford, then president of The Foursquare Church. At that time, I served my alma meter as LPC Vice President and was invited to become an individual member of the Connection, a relationship that has expanded and deepened my collegial and ministerial collaboration and development. Then, three years ago, I became president of LPC and have discovered an expanded benefit from my personal and professional affiliation with the Presidents' Network of the WHC. Dr. Mannoia's vision of bringing together various streams of the Wesleyan Holiness movement and to defining holiness within the contemporary context has brought about an impressive wave of resources for the church at large and for institutions like the college I serve.

During my career in college administration I have encountered students with a desire to live for Christ, yet who struggle with sometimes troubling contradictions of faith and lifestyle. These contradictions offer Christian higher education professionals a unique opportunity to confront, embrace, and clarify how we define holiness and ways in which our students, faculty, and staff interact with subjects that too often have become taboo for discussion in the church. The Wesleyan Holiness Connection shares my concern for the spiritual health and wellness of students and the professionals who serve them and has effectively opened channels of communication, compassion, and caring allowing appropriately responses with biblical fundamentals and a shepherd's perspective.

Dr. Katie Tangenberg, researcher and Connection colleague, recently presented important research on the campus discussions of lesbian, gay, bi-sexual, and transgender (LBGT) issues. Her unapologetic biblical exposition, coupled with the compassion of Christ as Saviour, healer, and sanctifier, offers a series of responses to the LGBT discussion that are particularly applicable to college communities. LPC Vice President of Academic Affairs Dr. Michael Salmeier joins me as enthusiastic WHC members and shares my appreciation for the work of those among our ranks who provide holiness-focused resources crafted with a high standard of excellence with the holiness distinctive.

LPC is grateful for the opportunities afforded it through the years to benefit our students, staff, and faculty as members of the Wesleyan Holiness Connection. Likewise, I am personally grateful for the opportunities afforded me to participate in rich dialogue toward a meaningful and effective application of Wesleyan-Holiness principles and practices in the twenty-first century.

#2 Sandra C. Gray, President
Asbury University, Wilmore, Kentucky

Asbury University celebrates with the Wesleyan Holiness Connection its first decade of ministry. We value our membership and participation with the WHC and find that the shared theological heritage and commitments provide fertile ground for membership discussions and collaboration.

Now beginning my tenth year as Asbury's president, I acknowledge the ongoing challenges of Christian higher education and understand more clearly with each passing year that leadership in the current environment requires a clear and consistent faith commitment. With the secular environment increasingly unsympathetic to our Christian worldview, even hostile at times, the WHC and its Presidents' Network is a trusted gathering of friends. Often the discussions tend toward the faithfulness of God where we can share, pray, and encourage one another. On other occasions the focus shifts to best practices in our mutual commitment to academic excellence and spiritual vitality.

The Wesleyan-Holiness theological tradition is essential to Asbury's approach to Christian liberal arts education. The Presidents' round-table discussions and exercises are especially helpful as we understand better that our work is not for purely selfish institutional interests, but to lift us out of ourselves into a larger sphere of thought and action so that we can contribute to the improvement of the world around us.

I deeply appreciate the way in which the meetings of WHC's Presidents' Network often engage and probe the other traditional institutions that are valued mainstays of society, the family and the church. Thus, this more comprehensive agenda provides a compelling program for each attendee to be free to explore many varied and penetrating issues of the day within the context of our Wesleyan tradition and our calling to faith-based higher education.

In November, 2014, a newly-formed Chief Academic Officers' (CAO) network of the WHC met in Portland, Oregon. Jon Kulaga, Provost at Asbury University, attended the meeting. A concern was expressed by many in attendance that WHC institutions were, by necessity, having to hire non-Wesleyan faculty. It was suggested that a retreat/workshop for non-Wesleyan faculty at our institutions be planned to help orient these newer faculty to a Wesleyan Holiness theological worldview.

In collaboration with the WHC and Kevin Mannoia, Jon Kulaga planned and hosted in September, 2015, the first such new-faculty retreat. This inaugural event included 38 faculty from six institutions, Asbury University, Indiana Wesleyan University, Trevecca Nazarene University, Bethel College (IN), Mount Vernon Nazarene University, and Anderson University. Speakers/Presenters included Kevin Mannoia (WHC), Chris Bounds (IWU), Joe Dongell (ATS), and Jonathan Raymond (retired president, Trinity Western University). Plans are underway for a second retreat September, 2016. This represents a tangible way in which the WHC can strengthen and expand the Wesleyan-Holiness commitment of our institutions.

Asbury University also participates in the Wesleyan Women's Holiness Conference. This is an opportunity for staff leaders to take students for a time of personal growth and encouragement in the faith. They describe the conference as a "refreshing time to engage with women from various backgrounds and denominations by coming together for the greater good of advancing Wesleyan theology and tradition to the next generation of women." As a result of the women's conference last year, one Asbury University student enrolled as a full-time seminary student and another is now serving in China.

A big "Thank You" is extended to the WHC for its faith commitment that is strengthening the present generation of Wesleyan leaders and growing the next generation.

#3   Shirley A. Mullen, President
Houghton College, Houghton, New York

It was no accident that John Wesley's original organization was called a "connection." The founder of the Methodist tradition wanted believers to be in partnership as they served our Lord. He also wanted the simplicity of "connection" rather than hierarchy, thus preserving the independence of each of the partners. It is Wesley's spirit of connection that has inspired the Wesleyan Holiness Connection in general and its Presidents' Network in particular. I am especially grateful for the work of the Presidents' Network. This informal association of college and university presidents from the Wesleyan-Holiness tradition has contributed to the overall richness of the Christian college movement, to the clarity of our campus missions, and to the encouragement of each of the presidents as individuals.

It all started as a time of fellowship during the larger Presidents' gathering of the Council of Christian Colleges and Universities. As presidents, we soon realized that we had in common a set of priorities and concerns. Furthermore, we realized that these distinctives of the Holiness tradition had not been voiced within the larger Christian College movement as much as those of the Reformed tradition. The task of articulating these distinctives motivated our group beyond pleasant conversation to a more formal agenda.

While our concerns do not make us utterly unique within the world of Christian higher education, there are characteristics that definitely mark our movement. First, we are marked by a commitment to translate theory into practice for the sake of improving the world. It is no accident that the Methodist-Holiness tradition is known for its impact on social conditions more than for its doctrine. Second, we are marked by our tradition of empowering women. It did not take long to realize that the women presidents in the CCCU were all from colleges and universities in the Wesleyan-Holiness tradition. Third, the tradition is marked by a hopefulness about the human condition. While we share the orthodox Christian belief in the fall, we also are shaped by our belief in the powerful agency of human free will under the guidance of the Holy Spirit.

The gathering of the Wesleyan-Holiness presidents has more recently inspired a similar gathering of presidents in the Reformed tradition during the CCCU Presidents' gathering. The sharpened articulation of the rich diversity within an overall Christian commitment to Christ-centered higher education can only strengthen the work of the Christian college movement.

This clarification of our distinctives soon began to move beyond collegial conversations at the CCCU Presidents' gathering back to our campuses. As Houghton's president, I became more intentional in thinking about how the holiness tradition ought to shape both our philosophy of education and our approach to spiritual formation. Campus leaders welcomed the conversation. For Houghton this conversation helped us to reconnect with our roots in the aftermath of the Second Great Awakening.

For our founders, the work of the Holy Spirit in the hearts of human beings manifested itself in tangible impact on the world around. There was none of the false choice between personal and social holiness. At Houghton, this reconnection with our roots helped fuel the expansion of our educational outreach to new constituencies in the city of Buffalo who were thirsty for a Christian education. This educational venture of connecting refugee and immigrant populations with the empowering resources of Christian higher education has called us to a renewed understanding of what it means to live out Houghton's historic mission in the new circumstances of the 21st century.

Our campus also took part in a larger research project headed by scholars at Azusa Pacific University that attempted to determine how the Holiness tradition shaped the spiritual formation of our students. The very decision to participate in this project inspired our Student Life staff and the Dean of the Chapel to think more intentionally about future programming that reflected the distinctives of the Wesleyan Holiness heritage.

Finally, the WHC Presidents' Network has been personally enriching for me. Early on, I was asked to be part of the coordinating team of the Network. Through this process, I have been privileged to become better acquainted with colleagues who would not otherwise have crossed my paths. The result is my hope that the work of the Wesleyan Holiness Connection and its Presidents' Network can continue to flourish. We are at our best when we are seeking to enliven and enrich the larger work of Christ's Kingdom in the world with the practical, hopeful, and transforming message of personal and social holiness empowered by the Holy Spirit.

#4   John S. Pistole, President
Anderson University, Anderson, Indiana

Being a non-traditional president of a prominent Christian university has its benefits and its challenges, personally and institutionally. Responding to God's call to such a role at Anderson University has been a new and so far fascinating journey. My entire career had been in non-academic pursuits, first as an attorney in my hometown of Anderson, Indiana, and then over thirty-one years with the federal government, including with the FBI and finally being nominated by President Obama and confirmed by the Senate as head of the Transportation Security Administration.

Although I led the TSA's 60,000 employees and headed up the counter-terrorism efforts of the FBI after 9/11, I realized that being president of a small Christian liberal arts college would have new challenges and joys. I have always sensed my roles as calls of God to public service. The prior four Anderson presidents had been ordained ministers in the Church of God and the last three had terminal degrees in higher education. Although I had my Juris Doctorate (JD) and was the son of a Church of God pastor/theology professor on the Anderson campus, I would be totally dependent on God's discernment, encouragement, wisdom, and strength.

One of the great joys of becoming president has been learning of the Council of Christian Colleges and Universities (CCCU), a network of believers who serve in leadership at other Christian colleges and universities. My wife and I were privileged to participate in the new presidents' and spouses' program in January, 2015, before we assumed our new responsibilities. We then participated in the 2016 CCCU conference and I also was able to participate in the Wesleyan Holiness Connection's meeting of presidents that preceded that meeting. What a special joy that was!

I met the presidents of many WHC-related schools and heard about the issues with which they were wrestling. Even though we may have different perspectives on specific issues, knowing that we share a common Wesleyan heritage and tradition quickly transcends those differences. We know that we are all part of the body of Christ, called to do our part in helping bring about God's Kingdom, being enriched by a Christian tradition so supportive of the best in higher education. I was also pleased to learn about Anderson University's key role in the WHC, including the role that retired AU professor Dr. Barry L. Callen played in the beginnings of the WHC and his current role as Editor of Aldersgate Press, the WHC's publishing arm. It was encouraging to read the literature of the WHC and particularly learn about the numerous books and articles authored by Anderson professors.

Now that I have been AU president for one year, I have learned to value even more these relational opportunities with other Christian leaders in higher education. As our colleges and universities deal with their identities as faith-based schools with changing societal norms all around, I believe the WHC has a God-given opportunity to be light and salt in a hurting world. In my governmental work, I dealt extensively with the challenges presented by terrorists who constantly adapt techniques to wreak havoc wherever they can. I have found a similar calling and challenge in Christian higher education, not dealing with terrorists, of course, but with the reality of living in a fallen, broken world in desperate need of a Savior. I heartily support the work of the WHC in helping equip the next generation of leaders in this pursuit.

#5 Henry Walter Spaulding II, President
Mount Vernon Nazarene University, Mount Vernon, Ohio

While I have attended only one session of the Presidents' Network of the Wesleyan-Holiness Connection, I was excited to experience the enthusiasm in that room. My comments will reflect what I see as the possibilities of the Network for this Connection in the future, with particular attention to its importance for higher education.

The Presidents' Network can assist in the broadening of resources available for theological development. The Reformed, Thomistic, and

Fundamentalistic Christian traditions have well-defined communities for theological conversation. The Presidents' Network can be instrumental in facilitating an academically rigorous, creative, and energetic community for scholarship, publishing, and teaching. From the start, we must acknowledge that the Wesleyan-Holiness theology is a vital part of the Christian theological tradition.

Three markers for engaging in a vital Wesleyan-Holiness conversation with the intellectual and social realities of our time are: 1. Understanding; 2. Human Nature; and 3. Moral Values.

1. Understanding is important to life for every human being. This is more than accumulating facts. Rather, understanding comes when what we know transforms the manner in which we live in the world. Therefore, we understand when our knowledge troubles the world of our assumptions. Paul gets at this in First Corinthians: "But we speak God's wisdom, secret and hidden, which God decreed before the ages for our glory" (2:7). He is talking about the Cross and Jesus. We might go so far as to suggest that we will never understand fully until we see all things through the Christ event.

2. Human nature is another marker for practicing Wesleyan-Holiness theology. It is almost secular orthodoxy to believe that human beings are little more than the most evolved species in the world. Some speculate about artificial intelligence and the idea that robots could one day replace human beings. Some speculate that other races in the universe may have evolved further. The conviction that human beings are created in the image of God is crucial for understanding human nature. When a Wesleyan-Holiness university seeks to educate students, it does so in the recognition that

human beings are "creatures with a human face." The psalmist put it this way. "Yet you have made them a little lower than God, and crowned them with glory and honor" (8:5). We live out our vocation in the realization that God empowers human beings to reflect God's glory in the world. Therefore, we repudiate any theory in natural or social science that misses the self-transcendence of human nature. Secularity attempts to flatten the world, but the gift of Wesleyan-Holiness is transcendence. God calls us to locate our self-understanding in the God who renews us in His image.

3. Our moral values present another marker in our attempt to understand a Wesleyan-Holiness trajectory. Each generation must account for the narrative by which we form our values. Whether the concerns relate to sexuality, economics, politics, or the environment, as responsible Wesleyan-Holiness theologians the place from which we respond is always the Bible and Christian tradition. Paul writes, "Therefore, my beloved, just as you have always obeyed me, not only in my presence, but much more now in my absence, work out your salvation with fear and trembling; for it is God who is at work in you, enabling you both to will and to work for his good pleasure" (Philippians 2:12-13). Our theological tradition is not dependent on a subjective "values-clarification" exercise for direction. This may mean that we will live as "resident aliens" in our culture (1 Peter 1:13).

The Presidents' Network can offer a way to facilitate a genuine Wesleyan-Holiness conversation rooted in these markers. The following benefits are clear:

- The opportunity to build a community of leaders who have a vision for building relationships to encourage creative pathways for theological contribution.

- Mentoring young scholars in the theological disciplines. It would be extremely helpful to build bridges to the social sciences, natural sciences, literary studies, and the professional disciplines. The Network can provide invaluable service by linking senior scholars and junior scholars for fostering excellence and wisdom.

- Sponsoring broad-based gatherings to address issues where doctrinal and moral convictions shed light for deeper understanding.

- Publishing significant works that deepen and extend the scope of the Wesley-Holiness tradition. Such work might provide a broader platform for understanding the various intersections of faith and life.

The Wesleyan-Holiness Connection presents an opportunity to engage in intellectually generous discourse among like-minded people of faith. The Presidents' Network can assist in providing resources for this conversation. For instance, several of our newer faculty attended and greatly benefited from a 2015 seminar for the integration of faith and learning. John Webster writes, "If God is prevenient in all things, then God is prevenient in our acts of knowing, and so our knowledge of God is rooted in God's self-manifestation" (*Confessing God*, 19). Ultimately, the bedrock of all attempts to discipline our learning through the reality of God is located in the faith that it is God who seeks us. Therefore, our agenda is clear – bring all things into conversation with the creating, redeeming, and gracious Father of Jesus Christ. The Connection's Presidents' Network is a wonderful place to do just this.

WHC ASSOCIATED MINISTRIES

AMERICA'S CHRISTIAN CREDIT UNION

by Mendell L. Thompson and Fawn Imboden

See, I am doing a new thing! Now it springs up . . . I am making
a way in the wilderness and streams in the wasteland,

(Isaiah 43:19)

od is always doing a new thing and surprises us by using human agency. Such agents included five men back in 1958; four
Nazarene pastors and a local businessman. They shared vision and a
common heart for God's Kingdom. The new thing God was up to was
planting a small seed of faith in the form of $135 to start the Nazarene
Ministers Credit Union. How small the seed might be was not as important as obedience to a collective calling, God's plan for building His
Kingdom. Their part was faith and faithfulness.

There is an old truism, a cliché really: "From tiny acorns mighty
oak trees grow." From the seed faith of just $135 back in the 1950s
grew a highly successful, faith-based, financially sound Christian
banking institution with nearly a half-billion dollars in assets today.
America's Christian Credit Union (ACCU) sprung up and matured
over fifty-eight years. It always has been established and rooted in the
Wesleyan Christian heritage. ACCU's mission continues to this day,
resourcing and partnering with ministries and people that are faithful
to the Wesleyan holiness tradition.

Making A Way

In the early days (1958 to 1986), functioning as the Nazarene Credit Union (NCU), ACCU grew under the leadership of its first manager and president, T. R. Partee. NCU focused on the basics. It preached and practiced credit-union style banking characterized by excellence in service, quality, convenience, and value to the members. In mission fulfillment, it resourced clergy and members of Nazarene churches with a diversity of banking services. This meant self-sacrificial service, demonstrated care for others, and stewardship. God blessed its faithfulness. As the NCU membership base grew it was increasingly capable of resourcing its Nazarene constituency more and more.

Then in 1986, and under new leadership, God began doing another new thing. An expanded vision became a turning point. Building on its fundamental strengths, NCU introduced its church-lending program in response to an even higher calling. It continued to mature into no ordinary credit union, but a financial institution with a higher calling, pursuing business practices grounded in core Christian values inherent in holiness and championed by John Wesley.

> ACCU's mission is resourcing and partnering with ministries and people faithful to the Wesleyan-Holiness tradition.

To its service to thousands of members, NCU added Wesleyan congregations and organizations in need of loans for new sanctuaries, building additions, Christian schools, and an increasing diversity of capital developments.

In 2003 the NCU changed its name. With an ever-widening membership base and a decade of success in resourcing infrastructure projects of Wesleyan congregations and NGO ministries, it adopted the name America's Christian Credit Union. The new name reflected the reality of God's leading in new and expanding ways.

For example, ACCU has long championed the Children's Miracle Network (CMN). This remarkable initiative facilitates and amplifies the volume of financial gifts to children's hospitals helping sick and

injured children. More recently, two new "charities of choice" are bene-
fiting from monthly staff payroll contributions as matching funds. They
are faith-based, non-profit organizations, Neighborhood Homework
House of Azusa and Shepherd's Pantry of Glendora, California.

John Wesley stated two broad categories when speaking of
God's means of grace. Both help us to be faithful to God's Great
Commandment to love the Lord with all our heart, mind, soul and
strength, and to love our neighbors as ourselves. They are: (1) Acts of
Piety (prayer, scripture, worship, fasting, sacraments, and so on). Acts
of piety help us love God, appreciate the presence of God in our lives,
and reveal God's true identity; and (2) Acts of Mercy, those means
through which we love our neighbor (feeding the hungry, healing the
sick, clothing the naked, visiting those in prison, teaching the children,
and so on). Acts of Piety reflect inward holiness and Acts of Mercy
reflect outward holiness. ACCU aspires to be a means by which both
inward and outward holiness can flourish and spread throughout
the land.

A Way in the Wilderness

The prophet Isaiah's words describe where ACCU was when it adopted its new posture and branding:

> Now it springs up . . . I am making a way in the wilderness
> and streams in the wasteland.

A new name occasioned an elaborated vision. By the new seed of a
new vision, ACCU began further supporting John Wesley's desire to
"spread Scriptural holiness throughout the land."

The elaborated vision began implementation with ACCU's financial and administrative support of the Wesleyan Holiness Study
Project (WHSP). Over three years, twenty-four professors and scholars gathered from colleges, universities, and seminaries related to eight

Wesleyan Holiness denominations. By year three, the study group grew to represent thirteen denominations. Their discussions were published in a book entitled *The Holiness Manifesto* (Grand Rapids: Eerdmans, 2008). That was merely the beginning. ACCU continued its support as the WHSP was transformed into a new reality. The Wesleyan Holiness Connection (WHC) sprang up. God was doing a new thing and ACCU continued its role as a means of grace helping to sustain the WHC for the next decade.

The WHC was a natural partner for ACCU's passion to support congregations, institutions, and organizations that would "spread Scriptural holiness throughout the land." God was doing a new thing in a nation and a world that continues to look like a "wasteland" spiritually and morally. God was "making a way in the wilderness" by strengthening the flow of the Wesleyan Holiness stream of Christian faith.

> The WHC is a natural partner for ACCU's passion to support congregations, institutions, and organizations that "spread Scriptural holiness throughout the land."

The new thing, the WHC, may be found at "holinessandunity.org." God raised up ACCU for many reasons. Now the divinely strategic purpose is transforming ACCU into a resourcing means of grace specifically to support of the WHC and thereby to equip, encourage, and energize voices of the Wesleyan stream and its holiness message. ACCU has been privileged to share financial resources with the WHC and crucial staff time, particularly in the person of Fawn Imboden, ACCU's Vice President and Chief Development Officer.

A Source of Gratitude and Pride

We are both proud and grateful. Today ACCU is not only transformed, but also transformative. Members and ministries who entrust their financial assets to ACCU recognize this. Its transformative capacity is much greater in Kingdom terms than any ordinary bank. It is not the only Christian financial institution in existence, but after nearly six decades it has emerged as a leader among the nation's faith-based financial institutions. It is a sound home providing stewardship over the financial affairs of many Christian servants. It has high added value because it not only shares their biblical values, but also puts its beliefs into action through Kingdom building investments, now including child adoption financing for Christian families. The Apostle Paul, writing to the church at Ephesus, wrote: "We are his workmanship, created in Christ Jesus for good works, which God prepared beforehand, that we should walk in them" (Eph. 2:10).

Looking back over the past nearly sixty years from its humble, modest beginning to the present day, especially in the nearly thirty years that I have had the high privilege of serving as ACCU's President/CEO, I am proud of what's been accomplished. All glory goes to God. The whole time he planted the seed, nurtured its growth, and opened doors of opportunity to serve in new and creative ways. God has made ACCU increasingly fruitful and expanded its influence and impact in, on, and through other Wesleyan institutions.

The whole time God has used the means of grace of human agency: the ACCU board, staff, advisors, and friends who prayed faithfully for its ministry and mission. The staff was especially a blessing, a key to how God has moved us forward. I am so proud of them. Together we are his workmanship. We were created and shaped by Christ for good works. God knew ahead of time and prepared ACCU over time as we walked together with him.

As I reflect on the past and envision the future, I know we are just beginning. God is always doing a new thing and it's not all about ACCU. It's about God and it's about living in holiness and service with the ultimate aim of bringing glory to God. In accord with the Apostle Paul's prayer for the Ephesians (3:16-21), we understand that out of God's glorious riches He has strengthened ACCU with power through his Spirit in our inner being, so that Christ dwells in our hearts through faith. We know, being rooted and established in love, we may have power, together with all the saints, to grasp how wide and long and high and deep is the love of Christ. And we know this love surpasses knowledge.

We know such love is in our hearts, and we know God's reason. By such love we become holy, filled to the measure of the fullness of God. We know then that, with such fullness, God is able to do more with ACCU than we could ask or imagine. And we know that this has not been and will not be for our glory, but to prepare ACCU for greater service to God's Glory. The Lord is faithful and will do it!

CHAPTER 25

THE JUNIA PROJECT

by Kate Wallace Nunneley

> The Junia Project is an online community of women and
> men advocating for the inclusion of women in leadership
> in the Christian church and for mutuality in marriage.
> We believe that when interpreted correctly, the Bible teach-
> es that both men and women are called to serve at all levels
> of the church, and that leadership should be based primarily
> on gifting and not on gender.

The discussion about women's roles in the church has intensified
in recent years. If this debate hasn't impacted your church yet, it
probably will in the near future. I'd like to pose two questions that I
think can help churches successfully navigate this issue.

Question #1: Are you aware of the debate?

It is important to understand the fundamental theological difference
between the two prominent views. On the one side is complementarian theology which holds that men and women are created equal but
intended by God to have different roles and responsibilities. The distribution of these roles precludes women from ever holding positions
of leadership in the church and requires the unilateral submission of
women to the authority of their husbands in marriage. On the other

side is egalitarian theology which holds that men and women are created equal and are called to roles and responsibilities without limitations related to gender. Men and women are equal partners in ministry and practice mutual submission in marriage.

The problem with complementarianism is that men and women are not really equal if women's roles result in a permanent subordination of women to men. It's an "equal but" position similar to the "separate but equal" rhetoric of racism. It has serious consequences, not only for women but for the whole church and for the gospel message.

Complementarianism presents itself as the traditional and orthodox view, and accuses egalitarians of having a low view of Scripture, being influenced by feminism, adapting to secular culture, or being on a slippery slope to liberalism. But complementarian theology is a relatively new position, first articulated in the 1980s. The predominant view of the church before that was patriarchy, which held that women were not suited for church leadership because they were inferior to men, having lesser intelligence and being more easily deceived. Complementarianism attempts to modify the traditional view by conceding the equality of men and women, while still upholding male hierarchy.

Modern egalitarianism was also formalized in the 1980s, although its roots date back to the early church, show up again in the Reformation, and surface in the Western world as early as the 1600s with the Quaker movement. The egalitarian perspective continued into modern times mostly through the Wesleyan-Holiness and Pentecostal streams, supported by strong biblical exegesis (see B. T. Roberts, *Ordaining Women*). Therefore, allegations of being influenced by feminism and culture are unfounded, and the slippery slope label is undeserved.

Question #2: Are you aware of the consequences if we keep quiet?

The voices who oppose the shared leadership of men and women are loud and strident. They have made hierarchical gender roles a keystone in their theology and have strong criticism for those who hold an opposing view. They have been on the airwaves, publishing books and curriculum, putting on conferences, and teaching their theology of gender in seminaries and churches, mostly in the Reformed tradition and the Southern Baptist denomination.

Although the egalitarian position is robust, especially in parts of the world where Christianity is growing the fastest, strong denominational voices are missing in the debate. Individuals and groups like The Junia Project have stepped in to fill that gap by advocating and sharing scholarly research through social media channels.[1] But the sense we get is that leaders in denominations that hold to an egalitarian theology are just now looking up from their work and realizing what is happening. These voices and yours are needed in this debate.

Let's make something clear: *egalitarianism is not feminism.* The equality of men and women is God's truth taken into the public square, not a secular idea that infiltrated the church. It was holiness women who first had the courage to stand up for their right to speak because the Holy Spirit was leading them. The stakes are too high to keep silent. For instance:

- 100-200 million girls are missing from today's generation due to preference of sons over daughters, gender-based violence, and the killing of baby girls and fetuses.[2]

- Rape is a primary weapon of war, especially in some African countries.[3]

- More than 200 million girls and women today have undergone female genital mutilation.[4]

1   See www.juniaproject.com

2   It's a Girl Documentary: http://www.itsagirlmovie.com/synopsis

3   United Nations: http://www.ohchr.org/en/newsevents/pages/rapeweaponwar.aspx

4   World Health Organization: http://www.who.int/mediacentre/factsheets/fs241/en/

- Sex trafficking is thought to be the second largest criminal industry in the world, and more than 80% of the victims are female.[5]

Women are in desperate need of the message that they were created in the image of God, that they too were meant to rule creation, that they too have a place of prominence in the Kingdom, that they too can use their gifts and lead in the church.

> Junia is named an apostle in Romans 16, but her apostleship has been questioned throughout church history—how could a *woman* be an apostle?

The consequences of male preference and male-only leadership are not only seen "out there" in the world; they are also seen in the church. It appears that women make up the biggest group of people leaving the church, with a prominent reason being that they are not valued as much as men.[6] Women also make up a large percentage of Americans claiming "no religious preference" today.[7] All of this contributes to the church being seen as increasingly irrelevant and out of touch.

The Story of the Junia Project

I have heard many people talk about being "called" into ministry. Gail, my mother, and I often joke that rather than being "called" into this ministry, we were "kicked" into it. It seems like the Holy Spirit pushed us into action and then ran ahead of us. We have been running to catch up ever since. My family has always been involved in campus life at Azusa Pacific University. In recent years we began to notice that

5   U.S. National Library of Medicine: http://www.ncbi.nlm.nih.gov/pmc/articles/PMC3651545/

6   Jim Henderson, *The Resignation of Eve* (2012).

7   http://www.pewforum.org/2015/05/12/americas-changing-religious-landscape/

students were coming into college with a more "conservative" view of gender roles than they had in the past. This has also happened on many other campuses.

In the spring of 2013 we decided to give a presentation to the community on APU's historical belief in the biblical equality of women. From this presentation came many conversations on campus. We learned how prevalent complementarian theology had become, even in some churches that have historically supported women in church leadership. We heard stories of discouragement and confusion about how women's participation had been limited. As one young woman said, "we're told we can be anything we want to be when we grow up – except in the church." We began praying daily, "Lord, what role would you have us play in addressing gender injustice?"

The idea of an online community came up. There was need for a place to continue the conversation about egalitarian theology. We started with a Facebook group, but we struggled with what to call it. There is a woman in the Bible named Junia who is named as an apostle in Romans chapter 16, but her apostleship has been questioned throughout church history – how could a *woman* be an apostle? At one point, her name was even changed by translators to make her appear to be male. Most biblical scholars now agree that she was indeed a woman and an apostle, but the debate continues in the church. Junia's story seems to embody the debate about a woman's "place," so we called our group "The Junia Project."

In a matter of months the group grew from 50 people in California to over 1,000 people in 50 countries – we had hit a nerve. Today the Facebook group consists of more than 7,500 people in 120 countries. We're also on Twitter and Pinterest, and we run a website with over 2,000 blog subscribers. More than 100 writers have contributed nearly 300 blog posts advocating for the full inclusion of women at all levels of church leadership and for mutuality in marriage. We have been asked to speak at universities, churches, denominational gatherings, and conferences around the country.

204 · THE HOLY RIVER OF GOD

Junia Partners with the WHC

The development of The Junia Project over the last three years has gone hand in hand with our personal exploration and eventual embracing of Wesleyan Holiness theology. I began working with Kevin Mannoia at the Wesleyan Holiness Connection not long after The Junia Project started. I was introduced to Wesleyan Holiness denominations (and movements) not only through their doctrine, but through the way they lived out their beliefs.

We sometimes hear that "egalitarian theology is simply feminism infiltrating the church." But my study of the Wesleyan-Holiness movement revealed that the roots of modern egalitarian theology existed 250 years before the start of feminism in the Western world. From the beginning of almost every single Wesleyan-Holiness denomination (many featured in this book), women were preaching and teaching and traveling as evangelists![8] Furthermore, I learned that Holiness women *started* the feminist movement. The first women's rights convention in the United States was held in the basement of a Wesleyan Methodist church! It seemed I had stumbled upon a gem of Christian history.

Claiming the Wesleyan Holiness tradition as my own has been an incredibly life-changing experience. Now I confidently speak for The Junia Project and am honored to partner with the Wesleyan Holiness Connection to help denominations better live out their theology of women.

---

8   These women include: Catherine Booth, Margaret Fell Fox, Aimee Semple McPherson, Phoebe Palmer, Anna Hanscome, Anna Howard Shaw, and many others. See:

- Roger Green, *Catherine Booth: A Biography of the Cofounder of the Salvation Army*;
- http://plato.stanford.edu/entries/margaret-fell/;
- http://www.foursquare.org/about/aimee_semple_mcpherson;
- Charles Edward White, *The Beauty of Holiness: Phoebe Palmer as Theologian, Revivalist, Feminist and Humanitarian*;
- Barbara Brown Zikmund, "The Protestant Women's Ordination Movement" in *Encyclopedia of Women and Religion in North America*.

CHAPTER 26

WESLEYAN HOLINESS WOMEN CLERGY

by MaryAnn Hawkins

Wesleyan Holiness Women Clergy (WHWC) is a multi-denominational organization with a mission to encourage and equip women called by God to vocational Christian ministry within the Wesleyan/Holiness tradition. It seeks to nurture women clergy through education, networking, resources, and personal encouragement, and to advocate for women clergy in all aspects of church and professional leadership. It serves as a resource to our supporting church traditions. Our name speaks to who we are: Wesleyan Holiness in theology and praxis, Women (self-explanatory), and Clergy, ordained or licensed or exploring the call to vocational ministry.

Failure to Fulfill the Vision

The WHWC began with a few clergywomen from five Wesleyan Holiness denominations sitting around a dining room table in 1990. The women had been invited by Susie Stanley of the Church of God (Anderson). They met in the Anderson, Indiana, in the home of Juanita Leonard. Significant concerns had brought them together.

Through the 1970s and 1980s the number of clergywomen who were able to find a place of ministry had dropped to an all-time low; denominations who had historically supported women in ministry seemed no longer to be doing so. Given the initial strong affirmation of women clergy in the Wesleyan/Holiness movement, and the many women who had ministered successfully during its formative years, an examination of Wesleyan/Holiness clergy statistics by the early 1990's presented a far more dismal picture for women than would be expected. The only exception was the Salvation Army which has maintained a high percentage of women clergy.[1]

The theology for support of women clergy was still being stated by the Wesleyan denominations, but the practice no longer matched the statement of affirmation. Ken Hoke, General Secretary of the Brethren in Christ shared a statement in a June, 2000, press release that articulates the difficulty between theology and praxis for most of us in today's Wesleyan Holiness churches:

> . . .(we) are open to women serving in all areas of Christian ministry according to their gifting and ability. We do not make a distinction among female and male applicants for ministerial license and or ordination.

> The call of licensed or ordained persons is up to the local congregation or group seeking to have a person come and serve with them in pastoral or other forms of ministry.

> Women are encouraged to follow the Lord's leading as to their gifting and then pursue the appropriate places where they may be actively involved in ministry.

> These statements reflect our official position. I regret, however, that I also need to say that our practice has not been as open as our official policies may indicate. We have not had a significant number of women assigned in lead pastoral

---

1   Susie Stanley, "Women Evangelists in the Church of God at the Beginning of the Twentieth Century," in *Called to Minister, Empowered to Serve* (Anderson, IN: Warner Press, 2013, 2nd ed), 65-66.

positions. We do have a number of women serving in credentialed positions on pastoral teams.

I am grateful, however, for our official stance. It keeps the door open and keeps the issue of women serving in ministry at all levels of credentialed church leadership actively on the table.[2]

Organizing the WHWC

The need for *something* to encourage women clergy was the impetus to organize. From that first small group of clergywomen around a dining room table in Anderson, with financial help from their denominations, the first Conference for clergywomen was birthed. The year was 1994, the place was Glorietta, New Mexico. Over 375 clergywomen attended. Clergywomen came, discouraged by the low number of women in ministry positions in their denominations, but encouraged by the possibility of advocacy through this fledgling organization. Those attending the Conference issued a clarion call for continuing this opportunity for clergywomen to gather.

> The theology supporting women clergy is stated by Wesleyan denominations, but practice often fails to match affirmation.

A second conference was held in April, 1996, which led to "great denominational enthusiasm, reflecting a willingness to support and encourage women clergy. Soon Wesleyan Holiness Women Clergy was officially organized under the sponsorship of five Wesleyan/Holiness denominations.[3] Two other Wesleyan/Holiness denominations later

---

2   Ken Hoke, General Secretary of the Church of the Brethren, North America. 2000.6.13 Press Release. WHWC electronic archives. Accessed April 12, 2016.

3   Susie Stanley, "The Promise Fulfilled: Understanding a Wesleyan/Holiness Paradigm for Women in Ministry." Unpublished Paper.

joined to bring support from their denominations and were extended membership on the Board of Directors. The denominations with representation on the Board of Directors were: Salvation Army, Free Methodist, Brethren in Christ, Nazarene, Wesleyan, Church of God, and Evangelical Friends International.

> The WHWC nurtures women clergy and advocates for them in all aspects of church and professional leadership.

Soon the Wesleyan Holiness Connection was actively affirming the work of the WHWC. Such affirmation became expressed by an action of the WHC admitting the officers of the WHWC to membership in its national Steering Committee, ensuring that the concerns of women clergy would be given proper prominence in the work of this larger connectional body.

Gift-Based Leadership

Having women preach and teach, lead worship, etc., was not a "new thing" for the Wesleyan/Holiness denominations. Allowing women in the pulpit was not a response to the feminist movement or even suffrage. No, it has been in the very fabric or Wesleyan DNA to allow those called by God and gifted by God to fulfill their obligation of service to the Kingdom of God. Vocational ministry is understood to be for those who are called and gifted, regardless of gender, race/ethnicity, or economic status. Note this from a theologian of the Church of God (Anderson) nearly a century ago:

> Again, I call your attention to the organization of the church by the Holy Spirit. A man is an evangelist because he has the gift of evangelizing. It is not because he is a man, but because he has that particular gift. The gift itself is the proof of his calling. If a woman has divine gifts fitting her for a particular work in the church, that is the proof, and the only proof

needed, that that is her place. Any other basis of qualification than divine gifts is superficial and arbitrary and ignores the divine plan of organization and government in the church.[4]

Being reminded of the heritage of gift-based leadership rather than gender qualifications, several denominations passed resolutions or made statements of support at their national gatherings. The difficult outcomes, however, have been that the numbers of clergywomen in pastoral leadership roles has continued to dwindle.

One feature of most Wesleyan/Holiness denominations is their commitment to a congregational style of leadership. In other words, each congregation may call its own pastor/minister. Even in those denominations that "place" pastors, only the Salvation Army places pastors without a congregational vote of acceptance. One may wonder if this directly relates to the Salvation Army's wonderful record of support and placement of women clergy.

So, what of the other Wesleyan Holiness denominations? Is the issue at the congregational level? Is the hesitancy of calling a female to congregational leadership related to cultural changes? Are there ethical issues in rejecting women from congregational leadership? In response to the ethical question, Cheryl Sanders states:

> In view of the ethics of holiness and unity, the privileged status of the white male in the Church of God is called into serious question. If holiness is our method and unity is our goal, then our ethical practices ought to be governed by the fruitfulness, love, truthfulness, righteousness, compassion, and forgiveness that set us apart as the holy people of a holy God.[5]

---

4   F. G. Smith, "Editorial," *Gospel Trumpet*, October 14, 1920, 2.

5   Cheryl Sanders "Ethics of Holiness and Unity in the Church of God," in *Called to Minister, Empowered to Serve* (2nd ed., Anderson, IN: Warner Press, 2013).

The Wesleyan Holiness Women Clergy has waved high the banner of gender inclusion. We have followed in the footsteps of biblical women leaders, of women throughout Christian history, and we continue to serve as an advocate, resource, and voice for women clergy to this day. The Wesleyan Holiness Women Clergy holds biennial conferences involving approximately 500 women clergy from the sponsoring denominations and beyond.

Editor's Note: See chapter 32 for the statement on this subject that was developed and widely disseminated in 2016 by the Wesleyan Holiness Connection.

WORLD GOSPEL MISSION

by Hubert P. Harriman and Dan Schafer

World Gospel Mission rode the waves of the holiness message and movement from its very inception, seeing scriptural holiness as a doctrine to be believed, an experience to be received, a message to be declared, and a way of life to be demonstrated. These roots run deep in the heart and soul of the organization and continue to be a vital emphasis in its people and purpose. You see this in its straightforward statement of faith:

> In the salvation of the human soul, including both the new birth and a subsequent work of God in the soul, normally known as entire sanctification, a crisis, wrought by faith, whereby the heart is cleansed from all sin and filled with the Holy Spirit. This gracious experience is retained by faith as expressed in constant obedience to God's revealed will, thus giving us perfect cleansing moment by moment (1 John 1:7-9). We stand for the Wesleyan position.

Birthed in Divine Fire

World Gospel Mission (WGM) was birthed in the atmosphere and fire of the early American holiness camp meetings, with direct ties to the National Camp Meeting Association for the Promotion of Holiness that was organized in 1867. Through this movement, literally hundreds of camp meetings were established in the United States "for the promotion of holiness." Two young men, Cecil Troxel, a school teacher, and Woodford Taylor, were deeply affected by one of these camp meetings.

The date was 1899. The Camp Meeting was Bloomington Holiness Camp Meeting in Illinois. The evangelist was Dr. H. C. Morrison who served as president of Asbury College and also founded Asbury Theological Seminary. Troxel and Taylor were there and heard the message of holiness preached with clarity and power. A few weeks later, after searching the meaning of this great truth, these two young men determined to pray for the "cleansing and infilling by the Holy Ghost." Troxel later wrote, "We were crucified with Christ. An ocean of divine peace was let loose upon our souls. The work was done. We arose from our knees having covenanted with God that we would obey even if it meant going to some foreign field."

> The purpose of the WGM is to spread scriptural holiness to the ends of the earth.

That field would be China in 1901. They went with a determination that scriptural holiness was to be their driving message, but they found this was not the heart of the organization they were with. Returning to the States, they came in contact with Mrs. Iva Durham Vennard who would found Chicago Evangelistic Institute (later Vennard College). She was also on the board of the National Holiness Association (NHA). Through her influence and guidance, the NHA would form what was called the Missionary Department of the National Association for the Promotion of Holiness (later the National Holiness Missionary Society), and Rev. and Mrs. (Ellen) Cecil Troxel and Rev. and Mrs. (Harriet) Woodford Taylor were appointed as their first missionaries. The place was University Park, Iowa Camp Meeting. The date was June 10, 1910. World Gospel Mission, as it was later renamed, was birthed with the purpose of spreading scriptural holiness to the ends of the earth.

Burnis Bushong details a history of changes that caused WGM to finally become incorporated: "To simplify the handling of foreign property, WGM became incorporated in 1926 but retained close legal ties with the Christian Holiness Association. WGM board members had to be approved by CHA, financial reports were submitted to the CHA for examination, and annual reports were given at CHA board sessions. The president of the CHA served as an ex officio member of the WGM board. Due to possible legal complications, it was mutually and amicably decided that the two groups be distinctly and legally separated. This was done in April 1981."[1]

The Troxels and Taylors would return to China November of 1910. The work grew and matured, with holiness as the fire, evangelism as the fuel, prayer as the fan, national training as the foundation, and compassionate ministries as the face. By World War II, more than fifty WGM missionaries had served in China. Churches were planted, medical care was offered, schools were established and Bible Schools were formed – a common sequence of progression in WGM's expansion into other countries. George Warner, one of WGM's missionaries in China, would become WGM's first president in 1934. The fourth president, Hubert Harriman, led the organization into a partnership with the Wesleyan Holiness Connection in 2014.

WGM's greatest source of power was the formation in 1913 of Prayer Bands across the States, and its printed voice, *The Call To Prayer* (recently renamed "The Call"), first published in 1919. WGM was carried forward on the wings of earnest prayer by literally hundreds of these bands of prayer warriors. Prayer continues to be both a core value and practice of WGM. In this ethos, WGM would go through other open doors. In 1942 WGM had 40 missionaries and four fields. By August, 1948, there were 120 missionaries working on eight fields. The peak would be 23 countries, over 300 missionaries, the homeland

---

1   Burnis H. Bushong, *Reaching the Unreached Now* (World Gospel Mission, 1995), 6. Also see the book by the same author titled *The Best of the Story*.

support staff, hundreds of Men with Vision work teams each year, and other volunteer programs.

Global Partnerships

As with most mission organizations, WGM is blessed with some signature causes and partnerships around the world. To list only a few:

- South India Bible Seminary established in 1937;

- El Sembrador – a school in Honduras for underprivileged boys established in 1959

- The Tenwek Hospital site in Kenya, Africa;

- Kenya Highlands Evangelical University dedicated in 1960;

- Bolivia Evangelical University, opened classes in 1982;

- Kenya Africa Gospel Church, WGM's largest field, with over 1800 churches.

The WGM home office was first located in Chicago and then moved to Marion, Indiana, in 1952. From its beginnings, WGM formed strong partnerships and played an important role with organizations such as the Evangelical Foreign Missions Association (now MissionNexus) and the National Association of Evangelicals.

Partnerships continue to be a strong value of WGM. With WGM's heart and deliberate focus on wholistic/compassionate ministries, and with its community transformation concepts, it has sought to connect with movements and organizations of like-minded thinking. With its strong medical ministry at Tenwek Hospital, it has partnered with groups like Samaritans Purse and the Christian Medical and Dental Association. With the growth and maturity of its more established fields, WGM now enjoys a relationship that has moved from one of founder to one of partnership with its national churches.

This spirit of partnership has also been instrumental in bringing about WGM's partnership with the Wesleyan Holiness Connection (WHC). This relatively new relationship has brought WGM full circle, with its roots in the holiness movement and its heart for holiness. Though there may be different methods of worship and ways of speaking to that truth, member churches of the WHC are able to unite under this banner of "Holiness unto the Lord."

From this connection with WHC, the book *Color Me Holy: Holy God – Holy People* was written and published by the WHC's Aldersgate Press. Co-authored by Hubert P. Harriman, then the fifth president of WGM, and Barry L. Callen, editor of Aldersgate Press, this book is now available in three languages and is being used for the inspiration and training of pastors in the United States, Kenya, and Honduras. It represents the fruit of the partnership of holiness brothers and sisters around the world. This partnership was further strengthened in July, 2016, when Dan Schafer became the sixth president of World Gospel Mission. He had served for several years as a WHC board member and foresees a continued, growing relationship between the two organizations.

> WGM is blessed with signature causes and partnerships, including its relationship with the Wesleyan Holiness Connection.

A Bright Future

The future of WGM is bright indeed. It has become clear that God is moving in a new way and intensity to ensure that the good news of Jesus Christ reaches and impacts peoples who previously have been unreached. The restorative power of the Cross that is proclaimed by both

WGM and WHC is the message that drives the missionaries who serve with WGM – a message of the complete restoration of individuals to the image in which God originally created them.

This salvation message brings deliverance from personal sin, from the bondage of false religions, and from the consequences of evil and its effects being left unaddressed. For those trapped in hopeless religions, this message of the Cross and holiness is attractive and will be effective in reaching the lost and otherwise hopeless of the world.

The depth of the holiness message not only gives real power and penetration to WGM missionary endeavors, but it also gives real incentive to God's church to be involved in missions. As holiness people, we recognize that God has set us free and, as we rejoice in God's good favor on us, we recognize that we must give our lives to deliver the divine message to others so that God can also set them free.

WGM is grateful for a partnership with WHC that helps us proclaim this message around the world. The resources, support, and cooperative efforts of WHC make a real difference in our ability to fulfill God's call on us.

THE WESLEYAN THEOLOGICAL SOCIETY

by Barry L. Callen and Diane Leclerc

With a rising tide of interest in the formation of a theological society dedicated specifically to the exploration and advancement of Wesleyan-Holiness theology, history, and practice, the Wesleyan Theological Society was formally organized in 1965. Its charter membership came from the Methodist Church, Church of the Nazarene, United Missionary Church, Free Methodist Church, Wesleyan Methodist Church, and the Salvation Army. As William J. Abraham said in receiving the Society's Lifetime Achievement Award in 2013, "We belong to a noble stream of the Christian tradition . . . . This whole trajectory of faith and practice we have inherited from John Wesley deserves to be represented at the highest levels of the academy and at the forefront of Christian social and missionary practice."

One important goal of the new Society was to nurture young scholars in the tradition. But there was much more. By 1979, Society president Melvin E. Dieter was making clear that Wesleyan-Arminian churches and people needed greater self-understanding. The Society could provide this and also "increasingly serve as a means to explicating our relationships with other Christian traditions and the secular culture as well."[1] The more recent emergence of the Wesleyan Holiness

---

1   Melvin E. Dieter in the *Wesleyan Theological Journal,* 14:1 (1979).

Connection has a remarkably similar set of goals. According to its president, Kevin Mannoia, the Connection seeks to serve the church and world as –

1. A visible presence which serves as a reference point keeping the holiness message alive and thriving in the minds and ministries of our pastors and leaders;

2. A source of resources and connections that will empower pastors, scholars, and leaders to find deeper understanding of our heritage and commitment to relevant holiness in the 21st century;

3. A voice to the church that allows the holiness tradition and message to be heard and to influence the diverse mix of theological streams on the landscape of Christianity.

As the Wesleyan Theological Society celebrated its fiftieth anniversary in 2015, its membership had exceeded 1,000 members and its academic publication, the *Wesleyan Theological Journal*, had become one of the more respected publications in the theological world. Its half-century of life and accomplishments were chronicled in a special publication co-edited by Society leaders who also are contributors to this present work.[2]

In fact, the Wesleyan Theological Society and the Wesleyan Holiness Connection share many key goals and leaders. For example, five recipients of the prestigious Lifetime Achievement Award of the WTS have been central in the formation and functioning of the WHC. They are H. Ray Dunning (2004), Barry L. Callen (2009),

---

2   See Barry L. Callen and Steve Hoskins, eds., *Wesleyan Theological Society: The Fiftieth Anniversary Celebration Volume* (Emeth Press, 2015).

Donald W. Dayton (2010), Susie C. Stanley (2012), and David Bundy (2015). In 2016 the WHC president, Kevin Mannoia, was awarded the WTS Preacher/Pastor/Scholar Award and, from its founding to date, the Editor of the WHC's Aldersgate Press has been Barry L. Callen, the longtime Editor of the WTS's *Wesleyan Theological Journal.*

> The WTS nurtures young scholars in the tradition and serves as a bridge between the Wesleyan-Holiness tradition, other Christian traditions, and the secular culture.

There were also several members of the WTS involved in the first meetings of the WHC where the purposes of the Connection were developed and the "Holiness Manifesto" was written. These participants included past presidents of the WTS such as Craig Keen, Donald Thorsen, and Diane Leclerc. During the first three years of what would become the broader WHC, approximately twenty persons presented papers, engaged in crucial theological dialogue, and envisioned the Holiness message for the 21st century. Wesleyan Theological Society members have also contributed to the WHC's many "Pastor's Days" across the United States and its meetings with presidents of key Wesleyan-Holiness colleges and universities.

The visions of the WTS and WHC flow in a similar stream. One significant emphasis common to the WTS and WHC has been intentionality about recruiting and placing women and ethnic minorities in leadership. Both bodies are committed to women's ordination and their leadership at all levels of ministry in keeping with the strong support of women from the inception of the Wesleyan-Holiness movement in the late nineteenth century (see chapters 24-25). The Wesleyan Theological Society has also had strong interest in celebrating ethnic diversity, specifically reaching out to Hispanic, Korean, and Caribbean communities. The WHC makes a point of including various ethnic groups in its conferences.

Both the WTS and WHC are committed to the Holiness message in general. Barry Callen put it this way in response to his receiving the

WTS Lifetime Achievement Award in 2009: "I believe that the continuing progress of today's divinely-inspired journey of the Christian community will necessarily go through a holiness message, probed, retooled, proclaimed, and boldly lived." In his 2011 response to receiving the same WTS award, Howard A. Snyder said: "God still seems to be up to something through Jesus Christ by the Spirit, and it is exciting to be a part of it."

The visions of the WTS and WHC are similar, including the intentionality about recruiting women and ethnic minorities for leadership.

The very presence today of the Wesleyan Holiness Connection is vivid witness to this growing excitement. The message of holiness brings laity, pastors, scholars, and educational leaders together in their common desire to "spread holiness throughout the land!" Kevin Mannoia put it rightly: "In the process of trying to find the magic method for growing healthy vibrant churches, our people have fallen prey to a generic Christianity that results in congregations that are indistinguishable from the culture around them. Churches need a clear, compelling message . . . . Our message is our mission!"[3] Both the WTS and the WHC promote the distinctives of the Wesleyan-Holiness tradition and believe that they have a theologically founded and imminently relevant message for today's world.

3   See Kevin W. Mannoia and Don Thorsen, eds., *The Holiness Manifesto* (Grand Rapids, MI: Eerdmans Press, 2008).

THE FREEDOM NETWORK

by Kate Wallace Nunneley

The "Declaration for Freedom" (see chapter 34) was born out of a collective passion for setting the oppressed free. The initiators were people with a shared heritage in the Wesleyan Holiness stream of the church. The holy river of God is filled with energy on behalf of freedom and human dignity.

In April, 2013, Kevin Mannoia had asked me to consider coordinating a group of Wesleyan Holiness folks to address the modern scourge of human trafficking. He had just come back from a Wesleyan Holiness Women Clergy conference and was encouraged by the amount of interest he saw on this and similar subjects. I agreed.

Our first meeting was in June, 2013, at Azusa Pacific University. About 10 people from the Southern California area attended and Mannoia pitched his idea to start this cross-denominational anti-trafficking network. The idea was well received and we decided to meet again in September at Trevecca Nazarene University's Justice Conference, where more anti-trafficking folks would be present from the larger circles of the Wesleyan Holiness Connection.

The Trevecca meeting was amazing! About twenty-five people came to hear about this cross-denominational network. We mapped out what this group's goals would be, what our vision was for it, and decided we needed a short paper declaring our commitment to freedom.

By December the "Declaration for Freedom" was written and the synergy of the group was established.

Members of this Network have worked together on abolition work both nationally and internationally. Wonderful ministry partnerships have been made, and resources are being shared. In 2014, the Network became somewhat of a home base for abolitionists in the Wesleyan Holiness stream of today's church life. Every time the Network has met together, someone would comment on how it felt like home.

> The holy river of God is filled with energy on behalf of freedom and human dignity.

In 2015 the Network decided to host a joint conference called the "Freedom Summit." The Summit was put on by the "Set Free Movement" of the Free Methodist Church, but the workshops were mostly led by fellow Freedom Network people. It was a great time of collaboration and teamwork. The group is looking forward to joining together to get the Wesleyan-Holiness colleges and universities more involved in anti-trafficking work.

WHC RESOURCE DOCUMENTS ON TODAY'S CRITICAL ISSUES

The biblical call for personal sanctity places before us an obligation to embody in practical living the implications of Christ "in us" for the world. The fine ideals of the Christian saints of the past are of little value now as mere museum pieces. To be significant, they must become evident in our common life today. We must live "godliness" through responsible participation in our world, with all its ambiguities and difficult problems.

The sanctified life is one that springs from a heart free "to will with God one will." Addressing in God's name the moral-laden social issues of our time is an essential aspect of the Christian life. Accordingly, the Wesleyan Holiness Connection has been active in confronting key issues and sending forth position statements on them as they are seen through the lens of the Wesleyan-Holiness Christian tradition.

This WHC confrontation is seen in part in the 2012 publication of Aldersgate Press titled *Heart & Life*. Various authors speak directly in those pages to the issues of family life, sexual deviations, affluence, racism, the paradox of power, the empowerment of women, holiness and higher education, holiness and worship, Christian unity, multi-cultural mission, and end times. In addition, the WHC and its affiliated ministries have released particular position statements seen in this Section IV.

CHAPTER 30

HOLINESS MANIFESTO

Wesleyan Holiness Connection, February, 2006

THE CRISIS WE FACE

There has never been a time in greater need of a compelling articulation of the message of holiness.

Pastors and church leaders at every level of the church have come to new heights of frustration in seeking ways to revitalize their congregations and denominations. What we are doing is not working. Membership in churches of all traditions has flat-lined. In many cases, churches are declining. We are not even keeping pace with the biological growth rate in North America. The power and health of churches has also been drained by the incessant search for a better method, a more effective fad, a newer and bigger program to yield growth. In the process of trying to lead growing, vibrant churches, our people have become largely ineffective and fallen prey to a generic Christianity that results in congregations that are indistinguishable from the culture around them. Churches need a clear, compelling message that will replace the 'holy grail' of methods as the focus of our mission!

Many church leaders have become hostages to the success mentality of numeric and programmatic influence. They have become so concerned about 'how' they do church that they have neglected the weightier matter of 'what' the church declares. We have inundated the 'market' with methodological efforts to grow the church. In the process, many of our leaders have lost the ability to lead. They cannot lead because they have no compelling message to give, no compelling vision of God, no transformational understanding of God's otherness. They know it and long to find the centering power of a message that makes a difference. Now more than ever, they long to soak up a deep understanding of God's call to holiness – transformed living. They want a mission. They want a message!

> People today want to see the awesomeness of God's holiness compelling us toward oneness with a testimony of power.

People all around are looking for a future without possessing a spiritual memory. They beg for a generous and integrative word from Christians that makes sense and makes a difference. If God is going to be relevant to people, we have a responsibility to make it clear to them. We have to shed our obsession with cumbersome language, awkward expectations, and intransigent patterns. What is the core, the center, the essence of God's call? That is our message, and that is our mission!

People in churches are tired of our petty lines of demarcation that artificially create compartments, denominations, and divisions. They are tired of building institutions. They long for a clear, articulate message that transcends institutionalism and in-fighting among followers of Jesus Christ. They are embarrassed by the corporate mentality of churches that defend parts of the gospel as if it were their own. They want to know the unifying power of God that transforms. They want to see the awesomeness of God's holiness that compels us to oneness in which there is a testimony of power. They accept the fact that not all of us will look alike; there will be diversity. But they want to know that churches and leaders believe that we are one – bound by the holy character of God who gives us all life and love. They want a message that is unifying. The only message that can do that comes from the nature of God, who is unity in diversity.

Therefore, in this critical time, we set forth for the church's well being a fresh focus on holiness. In our view, this focus is the heart of scripture concerning Christian existence for all times — and clearly for our time.

THE MESSAGE WE HAVE
God is holy and calls us to be a holy people.

God, who is holy, has abundant and steadfast love for us. God's holy love is revealed to us in the life and teachings, death and resurrection of Jesus Christ, our Savior and Lord. God continues to work, giving life, hope and salvation through the indwelling of the Holy Spirit, drawing us into God's own holy, loving life. God transforms us, delivering us from sin, idolatry, bondage, and self-centeredness to love and serve God, others, and to be stewards of creation. Thus, we are renewed in the image of God as revealed in Jesus Christ.

> Holiness is both gift and response, renewing and transforming, personal and communal, ethical and missional.

Apart from God, no one is holy. Holy people are set apart for God's purpose in the world. Empowered by the Holy Spirit, holy people live and love like Jesus Christ. Holiness is both gift and response, renewing and transforming, personal and communal, ethical and missional. The holy people of God follow Jesus Christ in engaging all the cultures of the world and drawing all peoples to God.

Holy people are not legalistic or judgmental. They do not pursue an exclusive, private state of being better than others. Holiness is not flawlessness but the fulfillment of God's intention for us. The pursuit of holiness can never cease because love can never be exhausted.

God wants us to be, think, speak, and act in the world in a Christ-like manner. We invite all to embrace God's call to:

- be filled with all the fullness of God in Jesus Christ – Holy Spirit-endowed co-workers for the reign of God;

- live lives that are devout, pure, and reconciled, thereby being Jesus Christ's agents of transformation in the world;

- live as a faithful covenant people, building accountable community, growing up into Jesus Christ, embodying the spirit of God's law in holy love;

- exercise for the common good an effective array of ministries and callings, according to the diversity of the gifts of the Holy Spirit;

- practice compassionate ministries, solidarity with the poor, advocacy for equality, justice, reconciliation and peace; and

- care for the earth, God's gift in trust to us, working in faith, hope, and confidence for the healing and care of all creation.

By the grace of God, let us covenant together to be a holy people.

THE ACTION WE TAKE

May this call impel us to rise to this biblical vision of Christian mission:

- Preach the transforming message of holiness;

- Teach the principles of Christ-like love and forgiveness;

- Embody lives that reflect Jesus Christ;

- Lead in engaging with the cultures of the world; and

- Partner with others to multiply its effect for the reconciliation of all things.

For this we live and labor to the glory of God.

CHAPTER 31

FRESH EYES ON HOLINESS

Living Out the Holiness Manifesto

Wesleyan Holiness Connection, March, 2007

As leaders press forward in living out holiness in their ministry, the following represents themes they will need to consider carefully in future years. We offer this as an invitation to engage together in unity around the transforming message entrusted to our care.

Dimensions of Holiness

- Holiness has several dimensions. Within each dimension there are contrasting realities. It is important to embrace both elements of each contrast in order to experience and practice holiness in its completeness.

- Individual and Corporate: We are called to be holy persons individually and to be a holy people corporately. The corporate aspect of holiness which is prominent in Scripture needs to be emphasized again in this time and culture.

- Christ-centered and Holy Spirit-centered: The Holy Spirit's work within us leads to conformity to the person of Jesus Christ. Neither should be expressed without the other.

- Development and End: God has an ultimate purpose for each person, which is to be like Jesus Christ. Teaching on development in the Christian life should keep the end of Christ-likeness in view.

- Crisis and Process: A definite work of God's grace in our hearts and our ongoing cooperation to his grace are to be equally emphasized.

- Blessings and Suffering: Full union with Jesus Christ brings many blessings but also a sharing of his sufferings.

- Separation and Incarnation: Holy people are in but not of the world. Holiness requires both separation and redemptive, reconciling, and restorative engagement.

- Forms and Essence: Holiness always expresses itself in particular forms, which are the ways in which it is translated into life and action. But the forms must not be confused with the essence of holiness itself.

- How do you balance these contrasting realities in your personal life and ministry? Where do you see the need for greater balance?

Essence of Holiness

The essence of holiness is that God is holy and calls us to be a holy people. The challenge is reflecting Jesus Christ in a relevant and contextual way that transcends social location and diversity. Indwelled and empowered by the Holy Spirit, holy people live and love like Jesus Christ. Walking intimately with him overflows in compassion and advocacy for those whom God loves.

How can you effectively embody holiness in the context where you are now, personally and in ministry?

Catholicity of Holiness

Although differences have led to fragmentation in churches, holiness invites unity. God wants to heal – to make whole – the brokenness of people, churches, and society. The impact of holiness goes beyond boundaries of tradition, theology, gender, ethnicity, and time to affect people and institutional structures. The resulting healing unites all Christians in wholeness, growing up into Christ-likeness. The message of holiness involves conversation and engagement with others.

> The message of holiness often has been communicated with terms and paradigms not well understood today.

What conversations and actions do you need to engage in to bring healing to people, churches, and society?

Holiness and Culture

Holiness people, while themselves influenced by culture, must convey the holiness message within multiple cultures. Culture affects the holiness message and churches because we are socially shaped human beings. Culture challenges us to mediate holiness in ways that are relevant and transforming without losing the integrity of the message.

How do we exegete culture and subculture in order to achieve transformation? How might you embody the holiness message in your immediate pastoral setting?

Holiness and Community

Individual and corporate holiness require that faith communities pursue organizational structures, processes, and content that promote radical obedience to Jesus Christ. Holiness does not develop in isolation from other believers and faith communities that provide spiritual support and accountability.

What communal structures, processes, and content would help promote radical obedience to Jesus Christ, personally and in ministry?

Holiness and Social Concern

Social engagement is an essential incarnational expression of personal and social holiness. It includes ministry among the poor, disenfranchised, and marginalized. Holiness requires a response to the world's deepest and starkest needs. Social engagement is the continuing work of Jesus Christ in and through the church by the Holy Spirit for the world.

> The challenge is reflecting Jesus Christ in relevant and contextual ways that transcend social location and diversity.

Since proclamation of the gospel of Jesus Christ to the poor is essential, how do you embody the continuing personal and social engagement with the disenfranchised and marginalized?

Communicating Holiness

Christians live in environments of changing language. They must communicate a holiness message in ways that are clear, relevant, and winsome. The message of holiness often has been communicated with terms and paradigms that are not understood today.

What terms and paradigms could you use to communicate the holiness message in a compelling way?

A CALL TO FULL PARTICIPATION

Women in the Wesleyan Holiness Tradition

Wesleyan Holiness Connection, September, 2016

The Wesleyan-Holiness tradition of Christianity affirms women in leadership at all levels of church life because of the teachings of Scripture, longstanding tradition of empowering women in pastoral leadership, and manifest evidence of God's work in the ministries of women.

Challenges to Women in Christian Ministry

While Wesleyan-Holiness leaders, pastors, and scholars have affirmed women in ministry since the earliest days of the tradition, many outside of these circles do not. With the growth of high-profile pastors, social media, and contemporary tools of communication, many voices can be heard who do not affirm or even condemn women in ministry.

While these negative voices are not Wesleyan-Holiness voices, many churchgoers do not understand the harm these can cause. With easy access to teaching that condemns women in ministry, casual listeners may come to think of this as truth. As more women are called into leadership positions in the church, a culture of strict boundaries fueled by such teaching will penalize women and communicate that they are untrustworthy or even shameful because of their gender.

Stream of Wesleyan-Holiness Advocacy

The role of women in ministry in the Wesleyan-Holiness tradition began in a small but vibrant spring. While John Wesley himself did not ordain anyone as clergy, he broke from his Church of England tradition and first licensed Sarah Crosby. This was followed by many other women preachers who became part of the Methodist movement in England and were influential as participants in the revivals that birthed the larger Holiness movement. Phoebe Palmer, a Methodist in the holiness revivals, arose as a Spirit-filled preacher whose writings would affirm God's call for women to preach, including Catherine Booth.

This empowerment set the stage for the visible role that women would play in the Wesleyan-Holiness movement around the world. Despite early advocacy, the Wesleyan-Holiness stream of Christianity is now experiencing proportionately fewer women clergy than in the early days of the movement. Our heritage prompts us to name, cultivate, and affirm for congregations today God's call for women to become ordained clergy.

Scriptural Evidence

The Wesleyan-Holiness tradition maintains its belief in the equality of women and men based on the nature of humanity's creation and purpose as revealed in Scripture. In Genesis 1:27-28, we are told that God creates humanity – both male and female – in God's own image and gives humanity the mutual responsibility of caring for creation as God's representatives. God did not create a hierarchal arrangement between male and female, but rather instructs them as equal partners to steward creation.

A careful reading of Genesis 2 supports the equality of women and men as part of God's vision for humanity. Referring to the woman as man's helper (*ezer*, v.18) is not a statement about the status of the one who helps, for God is similarly referred to as being the human's helper.

God creating the woman from the man's side does not necessitate sub-ordination (v. 22) any more than the man's creation from the ground (v. 7) makes him equal to the animals who were made from the ground as well (v. 19). Neither can we affirm that the man's naming of the woman's gender in v. 23 signals rule or authority. Furthermore, the fact that the creation of the woman occurs last does not mean that she is subordinate to man and animals, for it could as easily be said that her cre-ation is the climatic point of the story just as humanity's creation is the apex of Genesis 1.

> God did not create a hierarchal arrangement between male and female, but rather instructs them as equal partners to steward creation.

The biblical account of human-ity's creation bears witness from the beginning to God's vision of equality in status between women and men. God never tells one partner to rule over the other. Nor is there any mention of God granting au-thority or leadership to one gender. Rather, humanity as a whole was created as God's image bearers and instructed equally by God to care for creation.

An imbalanced power dynamic between the man and the woman occurs first in Genesis 3:16, which states that the man will rule over the woman. Because of the disobedience of the couple, a struggle for control developed. She desired her husband, but he may/will rule her. The distortion of harmony between the first married couple was a re-sult of sin.

God responded to sin redemptively in many ways and ultimately through the person of Jesus Christ. A central aspect of this redemptive message entails the equality of women and men (Gal. 3:18) who are to live in mutual submission in the light of love (Phil. 2, Eph. 5:21). Accordingly, the Wesleyan-Holiness tradition upholds the position that women and men – both of whom are created in the image of God – are united in God's calling to be God's image bearers in the world, shaped and defined by the person of Christ.

Jesus Christ's Compelling Mission

To reclaim Christ's compelling mission of the kingdom of heaven on earth, where there is no longer Jew or Greek, slave or free, male or female, but oneness in Christ, requires a togetherness that may be scandalous, risky, and otherworldly in our present social setting. This mission roots in a vision of the kingdom of God already active here on earth. It requires surrender to a compelling mission that transcends our human thoughts and usurps our fallen ways. It demands the humility we see in Christ but cannot experience without God's grace and a mutual submission to each other.

To accomplish this divine mission, a theological understanding of the equality of women and men must be gained and lived. This mission is not to build something new, but to reaffirm an original mission yet to be fulfilled. It is to restore through Christ the first vision of God for women and men. The mission enables a unity where the equality of women and men is foundational and central. It envisions a church where women and men assume church leadership on all levels based on their gifts, callings, readiness, and character, not on their gender. Wives and husbands are to submit to each other in humility, caring for each other, each preferring and honoring the other. There is to be proclamation that the good news is for all, by all, and to all. This mission comes through us, is for us, and yet is beyond us.

> There is to be proclamation that the good news is for all, by all, and to all.

Empowerment of the Holy Spirit

Jesus Christ is the great equalizer, and the Holy Spirit is the great empowerer. We learn this from Paul (Gal. 3:28) and in Luke's account of the Holy Spirit's activity at Pentecost (Acts 2) where both sons and daughters prophesied. We also learn this by carefully reading complex texts like 1 Corinthians 14:34-36 and 1 Timothy 2:11-14 in the light of God's renewing work in the world. The ministry of reconciliation to which we are called in Christ and empowered by the Spirit is a ministry of witness to what Paul describes as new creation.

The ordination of women is one implication of the good news that new creation means that God has changed everything. As we see the Spirit's extravagant gifting of all people as a sign of God's new creation, we will see that the ordination of women is not about models and social constructs, but about learning to embrace the gifts God gives us in abundance. Such gifts are tokens of the new world God has made possible in Christ and continues to bring to reality by the impartial gifting of the Holy Spirit.

The Imperative of Integrity

As new creations in Jesus Christ, it is imperative that we live with integrity, putting away the structures, hierarchies, and constructions of the fallen world and living eschatologically, expressing in our words, thoughts, and deeds the values of God's arriving kingdom. Hierarchy based on gender is one such worldly construct that imprisons men and women alike in roles that keep them from living out the new life given them by Christ.

Recognizing that powers and principalities are dead because they signal participation in fallenness, and further recognizing that in Christ we are made alive, we:

- reject gender-based constructs as impediments that keep us from living out the newly created order;

- live lives guided by a vision of the resurrection of the body and life in the world-to-come; and

- live this life as if that world-to-come is present now.

Therefore,

- we reject sexism as a symptom of a fallen world;

- we reject racism as a symptom of a fallen world; and

- we commit, in word and act, to proclaim boldly a freedom
  in Christ that transcends such structures and limitations.

All are one in Jesus Christ. Our primary and true identity is our belonging to Christ. **Our access to church leadership derives from the calling and gifting of Christ, not from one's gender.**

CHAPTER 33

GRACEFULLY ENGAGING THE LGBT CONVERSATION

Wesleyan Holiness Connection, September, 2015

God is love. In walking with God, we seek to love God and our neighbor. Such love compels us in engaging this conversation. It is a journey of discovery for all Christians living out an identity of humble integrity and loving purpose after the mind of Christ. We seek no argument, rather to engage from a disposition of humility and love of neighbor, realizing our own aberrant, broken condition as we pursue God's hopeful vision for us. Until the day that vision is fully realized, we accept God's grace so that in the face of our deficiencies Christ may still be seen and glorified through us.

The Wesleyan Holiness stream of the church has a history of actively engaging the challenging issues of culture in constructive and compassionate Christian ways. Standing on the shoulders of our forebears who struggled with societal issues in reflecting holiness, we draw upon our heritage in embracing the opportunity for engaging yet another significant issue at a defining moment. We invite our people to welcome every opportunity to engage the LGBT conversation as one that belongs to all. Because we all suffer from the effect of brokenness, we confess that we have not always done this well, often allowing other motives to cloud our intentions and misrepresent our passion to reflect God's holiness.

While many starting points exist to begin this conversation, our engagement stems from the Wesleyan-Holiness stream of the church that underscores the central theme of salvation as restoration. Based on a Wesleyan-Holiness reading of Scripture, we reflect deeply on God's vision of wholeness for humankind; the image of God in us; the nature of sin and salvation; and the power of grace as God's principal help in daily living. Proceeding from that framework, our engagement in this conversation becomes consistent with who we truly are.

This is a conversation. It is not an answer to all questions. We call upon leaders to integrate this framework in the particularity of their situation with grace and love that is consistent with the Wesleyan-Holiness tradition and the biblical imperative to love God and neighbor. We do not put forward a sectarian voice to exclude or demean people, for we all are created in the image of God.

Bearing the image of God is unique to humanity. Abiding in relationship and intimacy with our God allowed humanity to reflect that image perfectly and clearly. Possessing the freedom to choose, we chose ourselves over God. This selfishness is the essence of sin. The result of that selfish choice is broken relationship with God. In this estranged position, the condition

> We seek no argument, rather to engage from a disposition of humility and love of neighbor, realizing our own aberrant, broken condition as we pursue God's hopeful vision for us.

of the image of God becomes warped and broken within us and in relation to others. The essence of sin is selfishness; the result of sin is separation; the effect of sin is brokenness.

God in love was not willing that any should remain estranged and eternally broken. Love compelled God to take initiative in reconciling people back into close relationship, ultimately through the singular way of Jesus Christ. In Christ, God is redeeming the world, thus allowing the image of God to be restored in us. As the image of God is restored on the way of salvation, brokenness is made whole and we are being healed.

Any evidence of brokenness in people is a result of the separation that exists between God and us. It may show itself in compartmentalization wherein dimensions of living are kept from being integrated as God intended – affect, intellect, will, and physicality. It may also manifest itself when one dimension of life shows inconsistency or incongruity with the whole. This warped image in us represents disconnectedness among the various aspects of who we are – physical, intellectual, affective, social, psychological, and spiritual. Thus, we fall short of God's vision of complete integration and wholeness in our lives. In light of this, we believe that a same sex attraction, bi-sexual, or transgender identity represents an incongruity among the component parts of how God has made us. That disjunctive existence is the effect of separation from God. It is so in no greater measure than any other effect that falls short of the wholeness God intends for us.

God's vision for the human family is a picture of complete integration and wholeness in reflecting the similarly integrated wholeness of God. Since that image is dis-integrated as a result of separation, we live under the effects of sin. In that condition, the human family is predisposed to choices that reinforce, defend, or justify ourselves. People with a gender identity that is not the same as their physicality, whether by personal choice or the result of physical or psychological factors, reflect this condition of a dis-integrated whole. Those with a physical attraction to same sex persons as an expression of their own sexuality also reflect the condition of the human family being out of sync as a result of our not reflecting the integrated wholeness of God.

Likewise, those with a propensity toward addictions of any kind, adultery, gossip, or overindulgence are living with the effects of brokenness because of separation from God. Each of these exemplifies dis-integrated, asynchronous human life that has fallen short of accurately reflecting God's own image within us.

We all stand on common ground under the effects of broken relationship with God. There is no hierarchy of sin. We all look to the efficacy of God's path back into reconciled proximity. That way of salvation for coming back to God is through one person. Prompted by grace, it requires acknowledgment of an inadequate condition – confession; it requires a desire to be made whole again – repentance; it requires willful reliance upon the work of Christ for salvation – justification; and it requires daily surrender to the influence of God's nature transforming our nature through the work of the Holy Spirit – sanctification. Everyone may walk this path. Whether we begin in a condition of stubborn independence, addiction, greedy self-consumption, or as lesbian, gay, bisexual, or transgender, we all fall under the effects of sin needing a path to restored wholeness that only God offers us.

We believe that presuming upon God to redefine this vision for us is selfishness. Saying that our condition should be acceptable to God just as we are and that God's expectation, vision, and desire for us should include our current condition, removes the need for grace and relieves us of any responsibility to seek healing from our misrepresentations of God's image. Changing God's vision for us is another form of self-justification that replaces pursuing God's holy intention in restoring the broken image in us. We know that God is forgiving, God is merciful, and most of all, God is love – so loving that God has made a way through Christ for us to be restored in God's image.

It is by God's grace alone that we may manage the influence of our fallen condition through daily choices that guide our behavior. Grace is the help that comes from the very presence of God, which meets us in our sinful condition. When we resist that grace, we are not allowing God to collaborate with us. It means that we are denying the need of any help from God since our condition is not in need of any remediation. By resisting this grace, we have found completeness centered upon our own vision of our own wholeness, relegating God's vision to irrelevancy.

Receiving grace means we accept the reality of our condition as being inadequate. It means we rely upon grace as compensation for our inadequacy for as long as we live under the effect of sin. It means recognizing that apart from the presence of God we remain as an aberrant image of God's vision for us. Accepting grace means acknowledging that our humble vulnerability to God's influence upon us is the only path to wholeness wherein the various parts of our being will begin again to come into integrity one with the other. Accepting grace is living with a sense of fulfillment that is not the result of redefining our wholeness but the result of the compensatory nature of God's grace.

Some may dispute the vision of God for us as a binary gendered vision. Some say that vision should be expanded to include other combinations of gender identity and sexual expression that are not necessarily hetero or singularly gendered. This is the crux of the question and one on which we appeal to the Biblical passages (knowing that some will dispute our hermeneutical interpretation) and Scriptural principles (knowing that some may come to alternative conclusions). To inform our hermeneutics and our understanding of Scriptural principles, we also appeal to our historic identity as Wesleyans for guidance. We apply our Spirit-led reason to these Scriptural principles and we appeal to the heritage of churches and believers that have preceded us and bequeathed to us a long-standing pattern of engaging knotty issues.

> Saying that our condition should be acceptable to God just as we are removes the need for grace and relieves us of any responsibility to seek healing from our misrepresentations of God's image.

Sin has affected us all without exception. We humbly accept our broken condition. We do not consider any sin greater than others. Nor do we exclude anyone from the ever-present grace of God. We acknowledge God's desire to restore the image of God in all people. We are fully committed to salvation through Jesus Christ while depending on the Holy Spirit to meet our every need. Our daily quest is for God to make us whole. The grace of God is sufficient for all our needs.

Can people who self-identify as lesbian, gay, bisexual, or transgender live as growing disciples of Christ? Yes. Would the church deploy into leadership one who is humbly appropriating God's grace in not living out the practices of that broken condition? Yes. Would the church raise to leadership one who is practicing those behaviors as an expression of that condition? No. This is also true of any who willfully practice behaviors that naturally flow from conditions that tilt our hearts from God's vision for us to represent the image of God faithfully.

What is it, then, that we celebrate and encourage? We celebrate the humble appropriation of God's grace to a broken condition such that God's image is being restored – albeit with moments of failure and stumbling. We celebrate the vision of God for us in wholly reflecting God's holy nature and the attainability of that vision when we find eternity with God. We celebrate the grace of God, which sustains us until that day and gives us the privilege of living as whole people while still bearing the burden of our broken condition. We hold firmly that people who identify as lesbian, gay, bisexual, or transgendered belong in the church because the church seeks to welcome all who seek the sufficiency of Christ for their inadequacy. Acknowledging the complexities of lesbian, gay, bisexual, or transgendered life, we encourage Christian leaders to reflect God's love, grace, and pastoral care in engaging the uniqueness of particular situations they encounter, always seeking to encourage people into intimacy with God through Christ.

We hold to the vision of God for people as gendered, integrated, whole, synchronous image-bearers who reflect Christ well. This vision anchors our journey of restoration. We claim God's grace as sufficient for the enduring misrepresentation of God's image so that we may still grow though that vision may not be fully realized while living under the effects of sin in this fallen world. We may live in wholeness in this growing and intimate relationship with God, not based upon redefining our condition as whole, but upon the love of God whose mercy and grace invade surrendered and humbled hearts to make them whole.

Therefore, as Christian leaders who walk with our own limp, we reach out with acceptance and grace; we embrace with inclusive mercy; we act with motivating love – offering the hopeful call of God to wholeness in restored intimacy through Jesus Christ thereby reflecting the holy image of God in greater measure.

HUMAN TRAFFICKING: "DECLARATION FOR FREEDOM"

Declaration for Freedom, December, 2013

The "Declaration for Freedom" was birthed by the Freedom Network of the Wesleyan Holiness Connection, people with a shared Wesleyan-Holiness heritage and a collective passion for setting the oppressed free. See chapter 29.

Compelled by passion to reflect the holiness of God in relevant and fresh practices, the Wesleyan Holiness Connection represents churches and leaders with a common heritage that informs our unified voice to the world. Casting off the limitations of restrictive rules as an expression of holiness, we embrace the divine call to wholeness and restorative living in reconciling all things to God. In response, the Holy Spirit brings freedom to the marginalized, oppressed, broken, and hurting, and justice to the injustices and selfish influence caused by sin, until all things are restored in God's reign.

As a relevant and particular emphasis to the Wesleyan Holiness character within us, we speak to the contemporary scourge of human trafficking and slavery as one aspect of the freedom we seek for all people in reflecting God's holy nature. We therefore set forth this declaration, to guide and inform our future and call all people to action.

- Whereas we serve God – Father, Son and Holy Spirit – who out of holy love hears and responds to the cries of the afflicted;

- Whereas we are committed to our holiness Christian heritage forged in the story of freedom for those who are oppressed;

- Whereas the church is called to become a people who embody a more hopeful alternative to oppression and injustice;

- Whereas the holiness of God reflected in us compels us to advocate for just and hopeful practices in all areas of life;

- Whereas Christian justice requires a deep commitment to both personal and corporate confession and forgiveness as steps to more just action;

- Whereas acting justly involves compassionate care for those in our midst, as well as listening actively for and amplifying the cries of the oppressed, naming boldly and denouncing injustices, and working humbly against the powers that cause injustice;

- Whereas we affirm that the pursuit of God's justice and reconciliation is at the heart of God's holy nature being appropriated through us;

Therefore, the Wesleyan Holiness Connection issues a call to respond faithfully to the prophetic imperative for justice that beckons every generation to act justly, love mercy, and walk humbly before our God, by entering in Christ-like ways into a movement for the abolition of modern slavery and trafficking.

We follow our Wesleyan-Holiness Christian heritage that includes:

- God freeing people from slavery in Egypt, which in-augurated a trajectory of abolitionism that must continue today;

- The prophets' special concern for the widow, orphan, and stranger;

- Jesus Christ's anointing to preach good news to the poor, release to the captives, sight to the blind, and freedom for the oppressed; his example of raising up women and valuing children;

- The Holy Spirit who guided a persecuted primitive church to combine resources for the common good, and who awakens the image of God in all people;

- John Wesley's ministry that first started among the poor, and advocated on behalf of those impoverished spiritually, physically, and in other ways; and

- Influencers of the historic holiness movement who risked position, reputation, and life while standing for the oppressed and marginalized in historic struggles for the emancipation of slaves, the rights of women and children, just economic systems, and transformational engagement of the church with cultural issues.

> The Holy Spirit brings freedom and justice to the marginalized, oppressed, broken, and hurting.

Built upon this heritage and call to holiness, we make the following affirmations:

1. **We affirm that the pursuit of justice, reconciliation, and freedom is at the heart of God's holiness being reflected in people.** We commit ourselves and our ecclesial resources to working for the abolition of all forms of slavery, trafficking, and oppression, and to participate in intentional networks, conversations, and actions that provide hopeful alternatives.

2. **We affirm that churches should faithfully respond to the impulse of God's holy love by working for God's reign to be ever more visible.** We are called to be faithful witnesses in thought, word, and deed, to the holy God who hears the cries of those who are oppressed, imprisoned, trafficked, and abused by economic, political, selfish, and evil systems and persons. God calls us to respond in humility with compassion and justice.

3. **We affirm that acting justly involves the compassionate care for those in our immediate surroundings and also being able to name injustice, and denounce the powers that cause it.** Acting justly and loving mercy have often brought the people of God in conflict with the ruling powers and principalities of the day. God's justice calls us beyond equal treatment, tolerance of one another's differences, or simply reversing the role of oppressed and oppressor. By Jesus' example, we are called to a justice whereby we are willing to give ourselves up for the sake of another.

4. **We affirm that Christian justice requires a deep commitment to both personal and corporate confession, repentance, and forgiveness as necessary steps.** We confess and mourn the church's complicity in the injustice to which it has contributed throughout history. We confess and mourn the church's complicity in the injustices to which we continue to contribute. We confess and mourn our sins of omission, when we fail to act in Christian ways in response to the injustice we see around us. We confess and mourn being caught up in the very oppression the church seeks to oppose.

> We must seek the abolition of human slavery and trafficking, thinking deeply, praying with expectation, and acting with courage.

5. **We affirm that we must advocate for just and hopeful practices in all areas of life.** Reflecting the compassionate hope of Christ and love for all people, we identify with the conditions that bring dehumanizing circumstances. We will speak for those who are not heard, and come alongside the vulnerable by offering practices that bring redemption, restoration, healing, and freedom.

6. **We affirm that we are called to become a people who embody a hopeful alternative to oppression and injustice.** We are called to reflect the holy God in holy lives, bringing justice in motive and practice to people, circumstances, systems, and nations. While we may not end all suffering, as the body of Christ we are compelled to bring the holiness of God in healing fashion to the redemptive enterprise of restoring all things.

7. **We affirm that as a collaborative network we must think deeply, work holistically, and engage locally**

and globally. Complex issues drive modern slavery; therefore, multiple solutions must be undertaken. These will proceed from the fabric of who we are in Christian community naturally flowing into what we do.

We therefore pledge:

1. To work separately and together, as individuals and institutions, consistent with our Wesleyan Holiness identity to serve with compassion and to prophetically challenge oppressive systems;

2. To support, encourage, resource, plan, and engage together in effective, wise, sustainable action;

3. To labor as a worshiping community, with Christ at the center, infused with the power of the Spirit as a movement of hope;

4. To think deeply, pray with expectation, and act with courage.

For this we live and labor until God's reign comes on earth as it is in heaven.